POLITICAL PROCESS OF BACKWARD CASTES (BCs) IN PANCHAYAT RAJ INSTITUTIONS (PRIs)

POLITICAL PROCESS OF BACKWARD CASTES (BCs) IN PANCHAYAT RAJ INSTITUTIONS (PRIs):

PROS AND CONS: A STUDY IN ANDHRA PRADESH

Major Project Report submitted to the University Grants Commission, New Delhi.
Financial Assistance Under Major Research Project in Political Science

By

Dr. Gooru Sreeramulu

KALPAZ

ISBN: 978-93-5324-649-5

First Published, 2022

Published by

Kalpaz Publications
C-30, Satyawati Nagar,
Delhi – 110052
Ph.: 011-47034999, 9811692060
www.kalpazpublications.com
E-mail: kalpaz@hotmail.com

Printed at: Gyan Press, Delhi.

Contents

Acknowledgement

I wish to place on record my deepest sense of gratitude to University Grants Commission, New Delhi for sanctioning Major Research Project under MRP in Political Science. Without the financial support, this challenging study could not have taken a concrete shape. I am profoundly grateful to UGC for giving me an opportunity to carry out an independent research work.

I acknowledge my everlasting debts of gratitude to Vice Chancellor, Registrar, Finance Officer and Special Officer Development Cell, Gulbarga University, Gulbarga for their help, cooperation and encouragement in completion of this research work.

I am highly grateful to Principal Secretary, Ministry of Panchayat Raj and Rural Development, Government of Andhra Pradesh for his co-operation and encouragement for doing this work.

I particularly, acknowledge my everlasting debts of gratitude to Chief Secretaries of Zilla Panchayats of Anantapur, Warangal and East Godawari districts of Andhra Pradesh for their guidance and cooperation in completion of this research work.

I particularly, acknowledge my everlasting debts of gratitude to the Staff of DRA, Zilla Panchayats, Mandal Panchayats and Grama Panchayats of Anantapur, Warangal and East Godawari districts of Andhra for their whole hearted support and kindness in providing me necessary data and information for the present research.

I will be failing in my duty if I do not record my gratitude to all respondents, Managers and Staff of Backward Class of Anantapur, Warangal and East Godawari districts of Andhra Pradesh for their assistance in completion of this work.

I also express my gratitude to all the Chairman's and Members of Zilla Praja Parishad, Mandal Praja Parishad, Grama Panchayats of Anantapur, Warangal and East Godawari districts of Andhra Pradesh whose spontaneous co-operation went a long way in shaping this study.

I also express my gratitude to all the respondents in the study areas Librarians and staff i.e., Bangalore University, ISEC Bangalore, IIM, Osmania University, NIRD Hyderabad and Kakatiya University Warangal for their cooperation and moral support in completion of this work. My thanks are due to staff of the Library, Gulbarga University, Gulbarga for their constant help in completion of this work.

My deepest gratitude is due to Smt. Sunita Dattatreya Mohite, Project Fellow for her commitment, sincerity and hard work in completion of this project work.

I also express my gratitude to Prof. B. M. Baeen, Prof. S. A. Palekar, Prof. C. M. Yatanoor, Prof. P. B. Rathod and Prof. Hemalatha Jayaraj for their help and cooperation in completion of this work.

I am also thankful to Prof. P. Hussain Khan, Department of Political Science, Kakatiya University, Warangal, Prof. C.H. Balaramulu, Department of Public Administration, Kakatiya University, Warangal, Prof. K. Srinivasulu, Department of Political Science, Osmania University, Hyderabad, Prof. M. S. Talawar, Department of Education, Bangalore University, Prof. Sangeeta Satyanarayana, ISEC, Bangalore and Prof. Ramaswamy, ISEC, Bangalore for their suggestions, guidance and timely help in completion of this work.

I am also thankful to my wife **Smt. Sangeeta** and daughter **Sahana** for their cooperation in completion of this work.

Lastly, I thank Mr. Rajshekhar, M. B., **M/s. Suman D. T. P. Centre and Xerox, Jayanagar, Gulbarga** for neat typing work.

Dr. Gooru Sreeramulu

Prof. DAYANAND AGSAR
Vice Chancellor
Gulbarga University
"Jnana Ganga" Kalaburagi - 585 106
Karnataka - India

ಪ್ರೊ. ದಯಾನಂದ ಅಗಸರ
ಕುಲಪತಿಗಳು
ಗುಲಬರ್ಗಾ ವಿಶ್ವವಿದ್ಯಾಲಯ
"ಜ್ಞಾನಗಂಗಾ" ಕಲಬುರಗಿ – 585 106
ಕರ್ನಾಟಕ – ಭಾರತ

Telephone : 08472 - 263201 (0), Fax : 08472 - 263205
Cell : +919880663201 & +919448213398
E-mail : vc@gug.ac.in; vcgug@rediffmail.com; dayanandagsar@gmail.com

Foreword

I am very glad that **Dr. Gooru Sreeramulu, Professor** in the Post Graduate Department of Studies and Research in Political Science, Gulbarga University has made a maiden attempt to bring out a book entitled **"Backward Castes (A Political Process in Panchayati Raj, Andhrapradesh)".**

The author has presented the existing social conditions in Indian society. It is important to highlight conditions under which the low caste people are experiencing even after 70 years of India's Independence. Because, in order to overcome the caste-feudal exploitation and for the protection of the rights, a number of lower caste movements came into existence during the colonial and post-colonial period. These movements have questioned the very foundations of the caste-feudalism to overcome the exploitation, social suppression and for the human dignity. As a result in the earth while state of Andhrapradesh. The political institutions including PRIs were captured by high social groups or Castes.

The book brings out the facts that before the amendment of 73rd Act, in Andhra Pradesh the panchayat system was working with the domination of Upper castes. The earth while Andhra Pradesh Gram Panchayat Act. 1964 and Andhra Pradesh Mandal Praja Parishads, Zilla Praja Parishad and

Zilla Abhivrudhi Mandals Act, 1986 was in force. The author made sincere attempt to bring out the facts and highlighted contribution of Telugu Desam Party and its founder Late NT Ramarao, former Chief Minister of Andhrapradesh. The attempt made by the Act of 1986 for providing reservations to backward castes in PRIs is the significant in the history of AP, which is analysed systematically in this book. This act is considered as the most significant in the process of political participation of lower social categories. The political participation of lower social categories began after the 73rd Amendment Act, and its obligation on the states the state of Andhra Pradesh passed a subsequent act known as Andhra Pradesh Panchayat Raj Amendment Act of 1994.

The author has also used appropriate statistical techniques to ananlyse the data collected such as percentage, average and cross sectional analysis. The socio-economic background of the respondents from the institutions of PRIs has been analysed with response to caste, social status, education, agrarian status and political background.

The author has presented the views in seven chapters. The importance was on Evolution of Panchayat Raj Institutions in India, Panchayati Raj System in Andhra Pradesh, Profile of Andhra Pradesh, Socio- Economic Background of the Respondents and Perception and Problems of Political Participation.

The conclusions drawn from the study are of great relevance not only to the academic but also to those in administration. So that they can turn their attention towards initiating effective legislative measures for the effective political participation of weaker sections in the working of Panchayat raj Institutions.

Prof. DAYANAD AGSAR

Date : 08.08.2022

List of Tables

Chapter – 1

Introduction

Without understanding the Indian society, its nature - social structure, pattern of land holding, caste structure, the problem of rural villages, it may not be possible to understand the working of rural local Governments in India. Since Indian society is based on caste system and consequent social inequality, only the people from higher social status used to be involved in the process of administration, directly or indirectly.

Social inequalities existed in the villages and these have continued for centuries. Under these circumstances, soon after Independence the concept of social justice figured in the Indian constitution. Thus, the Constitution of India made an attempt to provide equal social opportunities for the development of personality of all the people in the society, without any discrimination on the basis of caste, sex or race.[1]

However, social inequalities continued for a long time in the Indian society. The reasons may be several. The people from higher social strata had received education, and they controlled and managed land. They took up income - earning activities. On the contrary, the lower strata people were denied education, and they were deprived of their right to manage and control land. Thus, they were forced to take up low - income earning activities. Particularly in the villages the lower strata people took up supportive works for the people who had taken up agricultural activities, such as Carpentry, Blacksmith, Leather work, and labour.[2]

Due to the above-mentioned reasons the marginalised became the weaker sections of the society. Therefore, after Independence, India was one among the countries which went in for social and economic transformation of the rural population. As a preferred condition, rural development became a definite strategy for the improvement of the living conditions of the rural poor. In this direction the Government of India made efforts to solve problems such as poverty, ill health, illiteracy, and backwardness of varied nature prevailing in rural areas, by giving greater attention to the uplift of the rural poor.

Further, the marginalised sections, i.e., SC, ST, OBC have become an important component in defining of the development policies because of their socio-economic deprivation in the traditional society like India. The political involvement of the upper castes is still more in institutions like Assembly and Parliament. The reservation of seats was 15% in State Assemblies and Parliament. On the contrary there was no representation from the larger sections of the marginalised castes i.e., from the backwards. As a result of this, at present, political participation in India is limited to only a few upper castes. As they manage and control the political system, land pattern. The upper caste people did not mind in formulating and execution of welfare and developmental policies intended for the weaker sections. It can be seen in the failure of several programmes. Among these are Community Development Programmes (CDP) and National Extension Programme (NEP).[3] These programmes were implemented in tune with the upper caste people in the rural areas.

Balwant Ray Mehta Committee Report

In 1957, under the chairmanship of Balwant Ray Mehta, a study team was appointed. The purpose was to evaluate the functioning of CDP. While reviewing the functions of CDP Balwant Ray Mehta committee thought about panchayat raj system. Thus, the creation of panchayat raj system in India is purely by the intellectual contribution of Balwant Ray Mehta committee.[4] The creation of panchayat raj system was begun in India on 2nd October 1959 in Rajasthan, Andhra Pradesh, Tamil Nadu, Kerala, Madhya Pradesh, Orissa, Uttar Pradesh, Bihar, West Bengal, Himachal Pradesh, Gujarat, Assam, and in some union territories. The basic purpose of creating the panchayat raj system is purely to meet the local problems and to implement the developmental programmes. Balwant Ray Mehta committee recommended three tier system for panchayat raj. The committee gave the thrust on panchayat Samithi, which is to be established at block level. It is known as block level body. It is a statutory and executive body, comprehensive in its functions, equipped with necessary authority and in possession of adequate resources. The committee further felt that the panchayat Samithi must not be cramped by too much control by the government agencies. It is important to note that the committee had given importance to panchayat Samithi and neglected the other two systems of PRI's. Among the other reasons the most important reason was that the committee wanted to implement rural developmental programmes very effectively and without interference from political parties and groups.

Ashok Mehta Committee

An important committee which was appointed in 1977 by the new government at the center was Ashok Mehta Committee.[5] It was appointed to enquire into the working of PRI's and suggest measures to strengthen them to "enable a decentralised system of planning and development to be effective". The committee also suggested recommendations only with the intention of development in rural areas. It recommended reform and revitalisation of panchayat raj based upon the central premises of "linking institutions of democratic decentralisation with socially motivated economic development".

Both the acts thought of attempting to bring about rural development either by three or two tier system of panchayat raj institutions. They could not achieve the specified motive to a larger extent, due to the ignorance of the people, non-involvement of weaker sections, to whom the schemes are to be reached. The upper caste and dominant people of the villages intentionally diverted the schemes. Thus, the attempt of panchayat raj institutions in developing the weaker sections has remained limited only to the records.

In view of these, the Constitutional Amendment Act of 1992 was came into enforce in the year 1993 known as 73rd Constitutional Amendment Act of 1993. As per the Act a due share has been provided to the social groups that is OBCs for their political participation and to take up plans and programmes for the welfare of these sections. The 73rd Amendment Act on the other side opted several opportunities only to the people with better agrarian resources among BCs. Thus, the developmental programmes are not reaching to the lower strata categories among BCs and still they remain backward.

Origin of the Problem

The lines of exploitation in pre-British India, in terms of the production, extraction and accumulation of surplus, were structured through the caste system.[6] This identified a particular caste division of labour involving specific forms of hierarchy among the exploited, with at least three major groups identified in most villages: toiling peasant castes, most of whom were simply cultivators but with some village management powers held by a dominant lineage, artisans and service castes performing particular caste-duties within a jajmani system: a large caste of general labourers working for the village and its dominant sections and classes as 'untouchable'. Tribals and pastoralists outside the village were also among the exploited sections. The exploited as a whole included a very wide range of castes, the broad 'toiling caste majority'.[7]

The toiling caste majorities also known as the backward classes, which is a general term applied to three different categories of people who have been identified, they are the scheduled castes, scheduled tribes and other backward castes, which together constitute about one-third of the total population of India. Among three the other backward castes constitute, in terms of numerical strength and castes, more. The term other backward classes was widely used by the British administration come to mean 'Other Backward Castes' in administrative usage. It is used in the Constitution of India to designate backward classes other than the scheduled castes and scheduled tribes. Article 15 (4) refers to them as 'socially and educationally backward classes (SEBC) of citizens' and article 340 as 'socially and educationally backward classes'. Article 16(4) mentions 'backward class of citizens' and article 46 refers to 'the educational and economic interests of the weaker sections of the people'. No doubt, the constitutional recognition of the other backward classes as a category of public policy made it one of an all-India scope but by contrast it is a more nebulous category. The other backward classes were mentioned in the constitution in general terms. There were no all India lists drawn for the other backward classes. They were not separately enumerated in the Constitution, and in fact, one has to work with only a rough estimate of their population. Their position was sought to be defined in more specific terms by the backward classes commission.[8]

The Other Backward Castes also termed as backward classes in the policy matter and bureaucratic circles is having theoretical limitation. In fact, in the Indian context all the forward castes and dalits have got the class character due to their privileged and under privileged social and economic position, therefore, they may be characterised as the upper class and lower class or exploiting class and exploited class. The backward castes also come under the exploited category by the upper caste but in a different form. The backward castes are collectively exploited and deprived all the privileges along with dalits. But untouchability is not practiced in the case of backward castes. For practicing the traditional caste based occupations to provide goods and services to the rulers in particular and mass in general got the higher position than the dalits and lower position than the upper castes and they are highly heterogeneous and stratified with similar socio-economic backwardness and interdependence nature of all these occupational castes. The traditional occupation prevented them to come out of the social stranglehold resulting in continued backwardness. Therefore, instead of calling them as backward classes, it would be more appropriate to term them as the 'Backward Castes'.

Therefore, OBCs are defined as the producing classes in India either in agriculture or in secondary manufacture through household hand craft production or in guilds of the goods that were of common use for society or specifically for the ruling classes. All these sections of society were made up of dependent 'jatis' whether as peasants or agricultural labour or as artisans upon superior castes: dependence, in other words, were of the collectivities and not merely of the individuals. In other words the direct producers in India was of a 'collective' kind unlike the 'individual unfreedoms of the European serf or earlier of the slaves'.[9]

Socially deprived backward castes lived in a social limbo somewhere between the upper caste Shudras and the untouchables. The Other Backward Castes existed all over the country in general and in every village in the State in particular. According to Nomita Yadav[10] "the core of the other backward classes consists of peasant castes of various descriptions. Frequently they occupy a low position in the Varna hierarchy and they have in general been devoid of traditions of literacy. Further, since they have also lagged behind in the pursuit of western education, they are often poorly represented in Government jobs and white-collar occupations in general.

In spite of this, such castes sometimes occupy a dominant position in the economic and political systems of the village-life. Not frequently, they are small landowners and when they are numerically preponderant, their control over a village, a group of villages or even a district can be decisive. They are known as what Srinivas (1959) calls the 'dominant castes' ".

Since Nomita Yadav defining the backward castes, while keeping in mind exclusively the north Indian Yadavs, it may not be applicable to all the backward castes in the country. The author tried to project the homogeneity of the backward castes but it is contrasting with the existing reality of the caste stratification and heterogeneous character of the backward castes.

The caste stratification, the occupation division and its hierarchical nature always posed problems in backward castes social mobilisation. It is a vicious circle in the sense that stratification cannot be altered without social mobilisation and mobilisation is a problem due to stratification. It is this enigma that needs to be probed into get at the law of change of these communities.

In order to overcome the caste-feudal exploitation and for the protection of the rights, a number of lower caste movements came into existence during the colonial and post-colonial period. These movements have questioned the very foundations of the caste-feudalism to overcome the exploitation, social suppression and for the human dignity. Before, going into the analysis of these social movements, it would be appropriate here to discuss the political participation of backward castes in Panchayat raj institutions.

Before the amendment of 73rd Act, in Andhra Pradesh the panchayat system was working. The earth while Andhra Pradesh Gram Panchayat Act, 1964 and Andhra Pradesh Mandal Praja Parishads, Zilla Praja Parishad and Zilla Abhivrudhi

Sameaksha Mandals Act, 1986 was in force. Particularly, the attempt made by the Act of 1986 for providing reservations to backward castes in PRIs is the significant in the history of AP. This act is considered as the most significant in the process of political participation of low social categories. The political participation of social categories began after the 73rd Amendment Act, and its obligation on the states the state of Andhra Pradesh passed a subsequent act known as Andhra Pradesh Panchayat Raj Amendment Act of 1994.

The state of Andhra Pradesh adopted a uniform pattern of panchayat raj system viz., a three tier system of panchayati raj: (1) Gram Panchayat at Village level, (2) Mandal Parishad at Mandal level and (3) Zilla Panchayat at the District level. Further, the act also provided for the constitution of Gram Sabha for every village. Besides, the structure of panchayat raj system, the act also facilitated provision for reservation of people belonging to certain depressed classes viz., SCs, STs, OBCs and Women in all the three tiers of panchayat raj institution. As per the act, 33% of seats are to be reserved to OBCs in all the institutions of PRIs with a definite vision of development of these some sections of the society.

Inspite of the constitutional provisions, the people belonging to weaker sections are unable to work in the institutions of panchayat raj independently. Among the several factors the social system and the structure of caste in Andhra Pradesh have predominant over the activities of Backward Categories and control.

Thus, caste has long been an important dimension of social articulation and political mobilisation in the State. In the domain of electoral politics, caste assumed an active role as the basis of political grouping and the mobilisation of electoral support in the State. In terms of caste structure and articulation, the regions i.e., Telangana, Andhra and Rayalaseema display significant variations. The Brahmins, comprising a megar percentage of the population and ritually placed at the top of the caste pyramid, have historically dominated social, cultural and economic life. It is only in the early decades of the 20th century that we find a serious challenge to their supremacy, manifested in the form of specific caste articulations.[11]

The Reddys and Kammas, comprising of below 15% of the State's population, are the two politically dominant communities. Although the Reddys are distributed throughout the State, they are dominant in the Telangana and Rayalaseema regions. The Kammas, on the other hand, are traditionally dominant in the coastal districts of Krishna, Guntur and Prakasham; their presence in other regions is marginal. It is the control of these castes over agrarian resources such as land and water that has been the most important source of their economic and political power. As the major land-owning communities and occupants of important positions of a village, they have traditionally controlled village political life. Among the other peasant castes, the Velamas, Rajus and Kapus are important communities with considerable political significance in the State, although in numerical terms they constitute only a small percentage of the population and spatially are confined only to small pockets. While the Velamas are a politically influential land-owning community present in northern Telangana and northern coastal Andhra, the Kapus are dominant in East and West Godavari districts.

Thus, in two regions i.e., Telangana and Andhra the higher social categories among the BCs captured the positions in PRIs (Balija, Kapu, Velama, Raju, Munneru Kapu). In Rayalaseema there are two types of representation of OBCs in PRIs. Firstly, most of seats captured by higher social castes with in BCs, which is numerically less in number but with the better agrarian and economic resources along with the support of Dominant castes. Secondly, rests of representatives are controlled by Reddy, and Balija castes.

Political Participation

"Political participation" is a term having many meanings. It is applied to the activity of ordinary citizens and to the activity of political leaders. It is used to refer to many different kinds of activity: voting, campaign contributions, marching in May Day or Patriots' Day parades. A term so broad can lose its usefulness. We must begin, therefore, by defining and delimiting the meaning of political participation. It is not our purpose to present the definition of participation. We simply wish to clarify how we shall be using the term. This is the crucial first step in our analysis. The rest of this book shall be devoted to describing who participates in what way, and to explaining why they do so. But we first must understand what it is we are explaining.[12] For this purpose, it is not enough to define participation; we must also discuss how to measure it, since our analysis requires that we be able to say how active a particular individual or group is.

The problem of defining and measuring political participation is compounded by the cross-national nature of our work. We shall be comparing participation across a heterogeneous set of nations. Is there something called political participation that can be meaningfully compared across these nations? And can we measure such activity in ways that are comparable enough to allow parallel analyses in each of the nations? Before we proceed, we must face these issues.

What is political participation?

By political participation, we refer to those legal activities by private citizens that are more or less directly aimed at influencing the selection of governmental personnel and/or the actions they take, though this is a rough definition. It is adequate for delimiting our sphere of interest. It indicates that we are basically interested in *political* participation, that is, in acts that aim at influencing *governmental* decisions. Ours is a broad conception. We are interested in a wide variety of ways in which citizens participate in relation to varied issues. Many studies of participation focus on the vote. Sometimes by choice, sometimes by default (because other data are not available), voting turnout of participation and for comparison with participation, not as measures of participation.[13]

In addition, we limit our attention largely to participation vis-à-vis the government. The argument has been made that effective participation depends upon opportunities to participate in other spheres – family, school, voluntary associations, the workplace. A participatory polity may rest on a participatory society (Almond and Verba, 1963; Eckstein, 1961). We do not quarrel with this assumption. But we shall not attempt to describe and explain patterns of participation outside those that are more narrowly *political* – that is, aimed at affecting the government.

One last limitation in our focus is our concern with activities "within the system" – with "regular" and legal ways of influencing politics. This eliminates from our span of concern a wide range of acts – protests, riots, assassinations, all kinds of civil violence – through which private citizens might try to influence the government. This is not to argue that the latter is insignificant or unworthy of study. It is simply another topic. The activities with which we deal represent a set distinctive enough in origin and impact to merit separate consideration.

Our conception of political participation is clearly broad enough to apply to the set of nations with which we shall deal. In each there are legitimate channels by which citizens can attempt to influence government policy or the choice of government personnel. But the mere fact that we can identify "political participation" in each of the nations does not mean that we have solved the problem of comparability. For one thing, the nations differ in the extent of the rights of political participation that are available. Several provide guarantees of the full panoply of political rights: the right to vote in meaningful elections, the right to join and form political associations, the right to petition the government, coupled with the auxiliary rights of free speech, a free press, and free assembly. Austria, Japan, the Netherlands, and the United States fall within the category of nations that provide the full range of these rights. But even among these countries there are variations in terms of restrictions on political activity. Japan, for instance, has a rather restrictive campaign law barring activities such as house to house canvassing, signature campaigns, the distribution and display of campaign paraphernalia such as buttons or posters, and a wide range of activities that might "raise ardor" (Cuntis, 1971, pp. 214 ff). This makes it difficult to compare campaign activity in Japan with that in other countries where such activities are not proscribed.

The converse problem exists in relation to the Netherlands. Until 1970 one form of political activity – voting – was required in the Netherlands. Our study was conducted after the repeal of that law, and we were able to ask about voting participation in two post repeal elections. But there is little doubt that the law boosted voting turnout when in effect (Irwin, 1974), and there may be a residual effect raising voting rates above their "national" level without such a law. Since ours is a study of citizen activity, not of the legal restrictions on (or requirements for) such activity, differences across nations in what is permitted or what is required compound our problems of comparability.

Similar problems exist in relation to our other three nations. In India, the central government has from time to time suspended certain political rights in states it considers troubled, and democracy went through a two-year hiatus in the mid – 1970s for the entire nation. At the time of our field work in 1966-67, however, India could certainly be listed with the preceding four nations as a nation providing opportunities for the full range of political activities. In Nigeria, on the other hand, there was a fairly thorough suspension of such rights under military rule about the time of our field work, and such rights have not yet been fully restored. Our field work in Nigeria had been planned before but took place shortly after the suspension of political rights by a military regime (The field work took place in the summer of 1966). Our questions, however, were about political activities prior to this suspension. This creates problems of comparability. First, the suspension of political rights under the military regime may have inhibited respondents from mentioning past exercise of such rights. We cannot measure this directly, but the reports of political activity in our survey are sufficiently high to suggest that there was no serious inhibition. The second problem is more directly measurable. Due to the unsettled political situation at the time of our field work we could not ask certain questions about party affiliation or activity in elections. Thus, our data files are blank in relation to an important type of political activity, a fact that will limit certain of our analyses of Nigeria.

The situation in Yugoslavia is even more complicated, since it is a "democracy of a different sort." In terms of the full panoply of political rights, one would have to say that they are neither fully denied nor fully available. The franchise is universalised, and there are often contests for particular elective positions. But organised opposition via competing parties is barred. Speech and publication critical of the government is allowed, through only up to a point, and that point changes from time to time. At the time of our field work, in 1971, controls were somewhat more tax than in recent years. The Yugoslavian system provides, on the other hand, a wide range of alternative political institutions – local councils, workers' councils, and the like – that foster high rates of citizen participation.

These differences in institutional structure make comparisons of political activity across nations difficult. The problem is compounded by other differences across the nations. Opportunities to engage in particular kinds of activity may be inhibited by social and economic conditions as well. One cannot follow politics in the mass media where those media are not well established. One cannot put a bumper sticker on one's car if one does not own a car. In short, our seven nations differ substantially in the opportunities provided for various kinds of political activity.

Furthermore, even if the opportunities to engage in some kind of activity were equal (i.e., if it were legal to put a bumper sticker on one's car and car ownership was equal across two nations), citizens in one nation might have the habit of participating in that way whereas those in another might not. But the citizens in the latter country might be active in other ways – perhaps they display posters. To compare the activity in one nation with that in another one would have to tap the full range of political activities in each nation, establish that bumper stickers and window posters are somehow equivalent (and therefore worth comparing), and decide whether a single bumper sticker is worth a single window poster.

Thus, though our concept of political participation is broad enough so that one can locate some such participation in each of the nations, there are a number of complexities in establishing the equivalence of such participation. The legal opportunities to be active may vary and the kinds of activities that citizens choose to engage in out of those that are legal may also vary substantially from nation to nation. How then can we compare participation?

Our answer is that one can compare participation in some respects, not in others. The qualifications listed previously make it difficult to compare the amount of political activity in one nation with that in another. To do so, one would have to know that one had asked about the "right" set of acts in each nation, that is, that one had not asked about an act common in country. A but not in B while neglecting a common act in B. Though, we have tried to cast our net wide and ask about a wide variety of political activities in each nation (some acts that were common across nations, others that were asked about in only one or a few countries), we cannot be sure that we have covered all relevant acts. If we had asked about a different set of political acts we might have received quite different results about the amount of activity in one place or another (on this general issue see Kim, Nie, and Verba, 1974).

However, our main interest is not in determining whether there is more activity in one nation than in another. We are interested in comparing across nations in terms of the internal distribution of activity within each and in terms of the forces that shape that internal distribution. As we have pointed out in Chapter 1, our main concern is with the relationship between equality of political activity and equality in social and economic terms. This type of comparison cases somewhat the task of locating equivalent measures of political activity. We do not need to know whether Austrians are more active than Japanese, but rather whether there is more or less difference between relevant groups of Austrians than there is among equivalent groups of Japanese – on the basis of the questions asked in each nation. If we ask about a fairly wide range of political acts we should be able to carry out parallel internal analyses.

Our concern with differences within nations also cases the problem of differences across nations in the types of political activities that are legal. What is crucial to our analysis is, as we have said, that all of these nations provide whatever rights they do provide on a *universal* basis – to all adult citizens, with no sex, income, occupational, racial, ethnic, religious, or other limitations. Our concern is not with the opportunities offered to participate but with the differential use that is made of such opportunities by different groups of citizens. As long as whatever opportunities there are universalised in each of the nations, we can compare the internal differences in the use of these opportunities.

The modes of political participation

We have considered the question of the comparability of political participation from nation to nation as though there were some single and unified set of activities called political participation. In fact, we do not believe this to be the case. There are many ways in which citizens can be active in attempting to influence the government. By this we do a letter to a representative, vote, or join a community action group, and so on. Rather, we mean that there are alternative *modes of nativity:* that is, sets of activities that differ systematically in how they relate the individual to his government. The explication of these differences among the modes of political activity is important to our argument both substantively and methodologically. It is substantively important because, as we shall see, the processes by which individuals come to be political activities differ from one mode of political activity to another as do the consequences of the alternative modes of activity. To ignore these differences is to misunderstand some important characteristics of participatory systems. A consideration of alternative modes of political activity is important methodologically as well. If we can locate similar modes of activity in each of the nations, we shall have gone a long way in establishing the political participation across nations.

Our stress on the multidimensionality of political participation differs from the emphasis in much of the earlier literature on political activity. In that literature (Milbrath, 1965; Lane, 1959) political participation was considered to be a unidimensional phenomenon. The main distinction across political actors was the extent of their "activeness" – essentially how much effort they put into political participation. Individuals ranged from activists who took a full role in political life, through spectators who observed but did not take part, to apathetic citizens who neither took part nor cared about public matters. We do not deny that this is an important distinction; "effort" is one of our major dimensions of political activity.

In fact political participation is both uni- and multidimensional. There is an underlying "activeness" dimension along which citizens can be arrayed; at the same time one can make finer distinctions among the activists in terms of the modes of activity in which they engage.

Our work on the modes of political activity has been reported elsewhere (Verba, Nie, and Kim, 1971; Verba and Nie, 1972; Verba et al., 1973). The modes we have located appear with remarkable regularity in a number of follow-up studies by others, the similarity being more convincing because of the heterogeneity of the measures used in these studies. We present a synopsis of our analyses of the modes of participation in Appendix A as well as a summary of the follow-up work. Here, we shall simply summarise some results as they affect our argument.

Our approach has been as follows: In each of the nations we asked about a variety of specific political acts. We asked about voting in several types of elections, about a variety of ways in which citizens can take part in election campaigns, about various kinds of group-based activities within the local community, about attempts by the individual to contact officials in his community or outside of his community on various kinds of problems. In some instances we asked about different acts in different nations. The surveys therefore tell us whether the respondent has engaged in our more of the activities about which we inquired. Using these specific acts, we looked for "modes of activity", that is, clusters of acts that customarily go together – in other words, a citizen who performs one act from a particular mode will be likely to perform other acts from the same mode.

We expected certain acts to go together because they were similar on some more abstract dimensions of participation. The dimensions were: (1) the type of influence that was exerted by the act (whether in conveyed information about the actors' preferences and/or applied pressure for compliance); (2) the scope of the outcome (whether the act was aimed at affecting broad social outcome or a narrower particularised outcome); (3) the degree of conflict with others involved in the activity; (4) the amount of effort and initiative required for the act; and (5) the amount of cooperation with others entailed by the act.

Our analyses of the various specific acts in which individuals engaged went through several stages (Verba and Nie, 1972; Verba, Nie, and Kim, 1971; Verba et al., 1973; and Appendix A). Factor analyses of the various political acts produced modes of activity that were similar across the nations and consistent with our dimensions of activity. The four modes that emerged were:

> ***Voting***: Voting is the most frequent citizen activity. It exerts influence over leaders through generalised pressure, but it communicates little information about voter preferences to leaders. The scope of the outcome is very broad, affecting all citizens. This combination of low information about citizen preferences and high pressure on leaders with broad outcomes is what gives voting its unique characteristic as a blunt but powerful instrument of control over the government. Voting involves the citizen in conflict, since the electoral situation is by definition a confliction one – at least if the election is competitive. The voting act, on the other hand, is an individual act. And voting differs from other political acts in that it requires relatively little initiative. The occasion for voting is presented to the citizen in the form of regular elections; he does not have to create the occasion. These characteristics of voting are fairly obvious, but they are useful, for they highlight some contrast with other modes of citizen activity.
>
> ***Campaign activity:*** The next regular mode of citizen activity is, like voting, in the electoral process. It is participation in election campaigns. It is a significant mode

of action, for through it the citizen can increase his influence over the election outcome beyond the one vote allocated to him. Like the vote it exerts a lot of pressure on leaders, and for the same reason. But it can communicate more information about the participants' preferences because campaign activists are a more clearly identifiable group with whom candidates may be in close contact. Campaign activity, like voting, products collective outcomes. Unlike voting, it requires cooperation among citizens. It involves the citizen in confliction situations. And more initiative is required of the citizen than in relation to the vote; campaign activity is clearly a more difficult political act than mere voting.

Communal activity: This mode of activity combines two types of activity: individual contacts by citizens with government officials where the subject of that contact is some general social issue, and cooperative, non-partisan activities involving group or organisational attempts to deal with some social issue. Such activity is outside of the regular electoral process. It conveys a great deal of information to leaders. The amount of pressure depends on the influence of the participating individual or group. The goal is some social outcome. Though some such activity may be conflictual, much communal activity involves little overt conflict (See Appendix A). The amount of cooperation with others varies depending on whether we are dealing with individual or group communal activity.

Particularised contacts: Our last mode of activity involves the citizen as individual (or perhaps with a few family members) contacting a government official on a particularised problem – that is, one limited to himself or his family. Such activity combines high information but usually little pressure. It entails little conflict among social groups and little cooperation with others. But it does require a great deal of initiative.

The characteristics of these four modes of activity in relation to the dimensions of participation are listed in Table 3-1. A factor analysis of the specific political acts on our questionnaire was carried out in each nation and produced results consistent with these four modes. Where alternative modes were found, they were due to specific differences across the nations in participatory institutions or in the information that we could obtain. The alternative patterns were consistent with our overall logic. Deviations were found in Nigeria and Yugoslavia. In the first country we had been unable to ask questions about campaign activity. Our analysis, naturally, produced no such mode. In Yugoslavia, the absence of competitive elections removed the major distinction that separates communal and campaign activity in the other nations – the conflictual nature of campaigning. Items from our communal activity set and items that would have formed a separate campaign dimension elsewhere (working for the nomination of a candidate, for instance) formed a single mode we label "regular" political activity. In addition, we found that functional self-management activities (workers' councils and the like) formed a separate mode.

The fact that we find a structure of participatory acts consistent with our expectations–and, above all, that we find similar structures across our heterogeneous set of nations–is crucial to our argument. From a methodological point of view it provides some evidence for the cross-national equivalence of political participation. Further, the existence of a similar structure of political acts across nations provides us with the raw material to construct comparable scales of political activity to use in our analysis. Substantively, the differences among the modes are important as well. Our main concern in this volume is with the processes by which individuals become politically active. As we shall see, the processes differ across the acts.

We shall, in this book, focus on the three modes of activity that involve public outcomes. Particularised contacting, though an important mode of activity, does not have the systematic relationship to institutions and to social conflict that would make it relevant to our current analysis. The three modes of activity that involve public outcomes – voting, campaigning, and communal activity – differ in ways that are relevant to our model of political mobilisation based on the interaction of individual and group-based forces. Some modes of activity should be more susceptible to individual forces, others to group-based forces. The characteristics of the modes that lead us to expect this are the case of the act (how much effort and initiative are required) and the amount of group conflict entailed. Those acts that require a lot of initiative and effort on the part of the individual ought to be less amenable to mobilisation through group-based institutional forces. Individual socioeconomic resources ought to play a larger role. On the other hand, those acts that involve conflict across social groups should be acts that group-based institutions would be highly motivated to mobilise insofar as they need support in their conflict with others. Voting is an act that requires little effort or initiative, yet involves conflict with contending groups. This suggests that voting will be an act that requires little effort or initiative, yet involves conflict with contending groups. This suggests that voting will be an act least affected by individual socioeconomic resources and most affected by institutional mobilisation. It should be easy to mobilise, and institutions should be motivated to carry out such mobilisation. Communal activity is different. It requires individual effort and initiative but the amount of conflict involved is uncertain. We would, therefore, expect communal activity to be susceptible to the influence of individual socioeconomic resources, and we are unsure about how much it is likely to be affected by institutional mobilisation. Campaign activity falls in between. It requires initiative and effort and therefore ought to depend on the socioeconomic resources held by the individual, but it is also a conflictual act that institutions would want to mobilise. We should find it affected by both individual and group-based forces.

Review of Related Literature

Various research studies have been conducted to study the women, SC, ST, BC's leadership at Panchayat level in different states. The Panchayat elections that took place in the State of Madhya Pradesh in 1994, brought forward a large number of women, many of who belong to the Scheduled Castes and Scheduled Tribes and backward castes. Besides male members. The studies on political participation of weaker sections in the institutions of PRIs in India have attracted the attention of scholars from deferent disciplines such as Political Science, Sociology, Economics and Women's Studies. An array of scholarly works examining the weaker section's representation, their nature, the factors contributing for their success and for failure along with policy implications has been brought out. A review of certain important works is quite pertinent in the context of the present study.

The review of some of such literature related to the topic are G. Palanithurai's (Ed.) 'Empowering People' throws light on Panchayat Raj system, Panchayat Raj Movement and the status of Panchayat Raj system in India under various stages of innovations. '*Decentralisation and Local Politics*' edited by S.N. Jha and P.C. Mathur, deals Panchayat Raj System in India in general and gives us a knowledge about reforms, development of Panchayat Raj and its governance and the implications in scheduled areas P.C. Mathur in his book, '*Political Dynamics of Panchayat Raj*', deals in length about Panchayat Raj system in India from 1959-90. Adhishesiah (Ed.) in his '*Need for Constitutional Safeguards in Panchayat Raj in Karnataka today: Its National Dimensions*', dealt in detail about introduction of Panchayat Raj system, its effects and need for constitutional safeguards in Karnataka. Eminent experts in the field like B.S. Bhargav, C.R. Bada, and V.N. Toragal, regarding Panchayat Raj System (Karnataka) dealt with introduction, stages of growth, working and position of Panchayat Raj System in Karnataka, in general. 'The Power to the People' reflects

Panchayat Raj Institution in Karnataka published by Department of Rural Development and Panchayat Raj, Government of Karnataka.

Sweta Mishra (1989), in her book *"Democratic Decentralisation"*[13] reveals that, decentralisation is an ideological principle associated with objectives of self-reliance, democratic decision-making, popular participation in governmental affairs and accountability of public servants to the citizens. Decentralisation is essential to achieve the broad political objectives such as, promoting political stability, mobilising support and co-operation for development policies and providing heterogenous regions, interests and communities, with a task in the survival of the political system.

Verma (1990), in his article "State Autonomy and Democratic Decentralisation",[14] expressed doubts about the sincerity and faith of the central and state leaders in the philosophy of decentralisation. He regrets that states have been fighting with the center for more and more powers and autonomy and that too discretionary powers, not for democratic decentralisation but for enjoying and exercising more powers. Political leaders of the states have shown little concern over their own village folk. They have never realised the powerful heads, their existence role and importance of these local bodies. It has also been suggested by another writer that political leaders use these local leaders only as their vote-contractors and brokers. It has also been suggested by another writer that political leaders at the higher level must have deep-rooted faith and reliance in the capacity and right of the rural masses. No one should consider them as unit for self-government on account of their poverty, illiteracy, ignorance, sex, language, religion and other forms and backwardness.

Nagendra Ambedkar (2000),[15] in his book on "Panchayat Raj at Work", explained the origins and growth of panchayat raj institution in India and structural patterns of panchayat raj in Rajasthan. The author also has given importance to electoral system of the local bodies. Further, he analyzed the socio-economic and political background of the panchayat raj elite, their perceptions and orientations of various issues, pertaining to the panchayat raj institution, finally he analyzed the leadership in panchayats and the qualities, attitude of the leaders towards weaker section of the society.

Malviya (1956),[16] in his book *"Village Panchayat in India"*, explains the historical and ideological background of the gram panchayats in India from times immemorial. The author focuses as to how the village panchayats in this ancient country developed into a sound system of democracy in accordance with our indigenous traditions and culture. The author concludes with a suggestion that the village panchayats are not the relic of tribalism or feudalism but are the results of matured experiment.

Maddieka (1976),[17] in his book *"Panchayat Raj: A Study of Rural Local Government in India"*, discusses that the panchayat raj is playing a great role in certain areas, particularly in promoting social change, economic development and intelligent administration of representative government. But all these become a vehicle for politics nepotism and corruption. The author suggests that there must be co-operative voluntary associations, between private firms and individual and government agencies dealing with different aspects of rural development.

Asha Kaushik (1998),[18] in her book *"Constitutionalisation of Panchayat Raj in the Gandhian perspective"*, focuses on Gandhian perspective in the context of constitutionalisation of Panchayat Raj and contend that the attempt to realise "Gram Swaraj" through 73rd amendment is a hasty conception premise of the Gandhian framework. Basing her arguments on Gandhian ideas about state, place of individual in social life, and village panchayats, she makes a fervert plea to thinking terms of "democratic governance, which is not merely a structural arrangement of rights, but also a normative concern with civic and political obligations, as visualised by Gandhi".

Sammiuddin, Abida (1976),[19] in her book *"A Critique of Panchayat raj with Special Reference to Uttar Pradesh"*, examine the genesis and growth of Community Development Programmes in their broad perspective and has highlighted their relevance to rural economy and democratic institutions of Panchayat Raj. She emphasis on proper training of rural services and has stressed the need for providing job oriented education and training in social skills to the personnel, programmes and Panchayat Raj Institutions. The authors suggests that the grass root institutions need the revision of the basic objective of development programmes, structural reforms of organisational pattern, administrative techniques and adequate financial resources matching with their responsibilities.

Lakshaminarayan (1976),[20] in his book *"India's Villages at Gross Roots"*, focuses on the conditions and problems of rural people, their institutions and way of living under the impact of planned social change after the Institutions of the Community Development Programmes in Mandya District of Mysore State. These villages have been integrated with the wider economic and political system and have many linkages with communication and other Institutional network. The author opined that the improved means of communication, community development programmes and the Panchayat Raj have played a significant role in modernising the village. He concludes that the political set up has politicised the traditional society. But these have not affected the social structure of village.

Narayan's article (1998),[21] on "Panchayat Raj and Scheduled Castes, Scheduled Tribes and Other Backward Classes", discussed the empowerment of scheduled castes, scheduled tribes and other backward classes. The opined that though, their representation in new structures of Panchayat Raj has been the most significant issue of concern and attention. A lot of enthusiasm has been evinced, both by the deserving sections and by the scholars studying new phenomena. He has made a forceful plea for direct election to positions of Chairperson, at the intermediate and top levels of Panchayat Raj system and mobilisation of weaker sections. He rightly feels that any excessive power sharing would be in consequential if it is not preceded by land reforms and reduction of inequalities and end of exploitation. Finally wants political parties and NGO's to come forward and help the weaker sections by creating political awakening and effective mobilisation.

Gehlot (1998),[22] in his article "Toward Panchayat Raj: Some Myths of Democratic Decentralisation", discussed the historical aspects of Panchayat Raj and highlights the problem areas likely to emerge in the way of new devolution and decentralisation patterns. He advocated a motivated bureaucracy to gear up the task and devaluation of authority to elected representatives. Highlighting the dominance of vested interests, he makes a plea for providing Panchayat Raj Institutions (PRI's), much needed strength to deliver goods to the deserving ones. Issues of rural electrification, untouchability, discrimination and deprivation of scheduled castes and tribes and reluctance of state governments to share their resources deserve a serious consideration. He feels that creation of legislative council at state level to represent panchayats, according priority to land reform and strengthening MP local areas development scheme (MPLADS) can help PR to grow and deliver the goods.

Rao (1980),[23] in his book *"Panchayat Raj and Rural Development"*, states that the success of rural development through democratic decentralisation largely depends on two basic factors viz., (a) the emergence and growth of egalitarian power structure in democratic institutions at the grass root and (b) economically viable size of these institution. Therefore, the author deals with the investigation of these two issues at the level of village Panchayat in Tumkur district of Karnataka. The author comes to the conclusion that larger panchayats having a population base of 4,000 would be economically viable to implement rural development programmes. In this context, he suggests that such a unit of 4,000 persons should form the basis for Panchayat, a co-operative and other institutions dealing with rural development; a cluster approach has been suggested. Secondly, there is a need to give representation to villagers rather than to population within the unit so that each village having a population of at least 200 persons will have its representative in the Panchayat to take care of its interest. There is urgent need for effective implementation of land reform and improving the spread of education among the weaker section of society, as has been advocated by many authors. The dominance of the upper economic classes in panchayats and in other local level institutions is well known and is well-established fact, as already brought out by other research studies. Further, efforts are made to suggest how the local institutions can become more representative and how to ensure that the benefits of development could reach the weaker sections in an increasing measures.

"The report of the Committee to Review the Rural Development and Poverty Alleviation Programmes (1985)"[24] examined that structure and suitability of the institutional arrangement that have been made for the delivery of rural development programmes, especially to the poor. The study, therefore, also looks at selected programmes to observe the performance in relation to their stated objectives. The authors concluded that poverty and inequality are on the increase. The basic reason for the failure of rural development and poverty elevation programmes is the exclusion of the people from participation in the development process and abandonment of the institution of democratic decentralisation and the related electoral process. In the circumstances, the only solution is the democratic decentralisation.

1952 was also the year when the First Five Year Plan was started. According to the Planning Commission, "Community

Development is the method of Rural Extension the agency through which the Five Year Plan seeks to initiate a process of transformation of the social and economic life of the village.[13] In course of five years of experiment in Community Development, it was realised that it failed to arouse popular initiative and cooperation for development and welfare programmes.

Prasad (1971),[25] studied Twin Process of Democratisation and Development in Village Awa of Bihar, he concluded that while the village Panchayat has stimulated the process of political democratisation, it has not accelerated the pace of economic development in the villages.

Kumar and Venkataraman (1974),[26] examined the Administrative, Financial and Technical Aspects of Supervision and Control in Tamil Nadu. It has been realised that the way in which control is exercised depends very much on the linkage of officials and non-officials who are concerned with the Panchayati Raj movement.

Rai and Singh (1975)[27] study the Panchayati Raj System from Community Development Programme to Balwant Ray Mehta Committee Report and its implementation. They concluded that the present system of election is not conducive to the growth of healthy popular participation at the local level. To strengthen participation they suggest that the head of the local educational institution and office bearers of different political parties should be associated with the Panchayati Raj bodies.

Pant (1979),[28] tries to delineate the Sources and Areas of Conflict, Cooperation and Collaboration Between Officials and Non-Officials in Bhagalpur District of Bihar and also tries to find out the reasons of the prevailing state of affairs. He concludes that the structural reforms are not the panacea for the ills of Panchayati Raj. Placing the officials under non-officials might create problems of greater dimensions. There is a need of committed non-officials leadership and efficient, development minded officers. This can only be possible if the larger socio-political culture of officials and non-officials undergoes significant changes.

Darshankar (1979),[29] discusses the interaction between Caste and Politics Role of Money, Education and Social Rank in the Working of Panchayati Raj Institutions in Marthwada region of Maharashtra State. He suggested that success of Panchayati Raj largely depends on the leaders and they have to be deeply committed to the ideals of Panchayati Raj. There is a hope that with the emergence of sound snap enlightened and committed leadership in these institutions will function for the betterment of the rural community as a whole.

Sharma (1979)[30] hints at the links between the Rural Leadership and the needs of Villagers in Negotiations with the Urban Administrative Centers and Political Powers at Higher Level in the Western part of Uttar Pradesh. When leadership is viewed over a number of panchayat elections, continuity, discontinuity, re-emergence of leaders appear, caste remains the same, only individuals change. He says that these castes are the major landowners. The castes controlling powers have maintained their supremacy. Even the opposition comes largely from within the dominant caste and a limited number of Khandans act as operators of political powers whether in authority or in oppositions.

Bhargava (1979)[31] examines the achievements and Role of Political Parties in Rajasthan. He maintains that there is too much politics and the benefits of these institutions are only enjoyed by the leaders and their associates. These institutions are financially very weak and its members look after their self-interest and want to monopolies position and power. Cooperation is not forthcoming from the government officials and slackness and indifference have crept into the members because there have been no elections since a long time in these institutions. The role of political parties in relation to Panchayati

Raj system has not been satisfactory. Power Orientation' of political parties is understandable, but not at the cost of the functioning of the system. The author suggested that for raising the 'standards of politics' and 'performance improvement' of the political parties in relation to Panchayati Raj system, steps should be taken in the direction of its (system's) acquiring reasonable level of legitimacy.

Singh (1987)[32] presents a historical view of the Panchayat Raj institutions in India together with a Discussion on the Theoretical, Organisational and Functional Dimensions of the Panchayati Raj. He concludes that Bihar was one of the first states in India to enact a legislation on Panchayati Raj (1947), yet regular elections could not be held and devolution of power was not possible. The state government played with the idea of devolution of power as it pleased the politics administrative bureaucracy. The Panchayati Raj could not succeed even in eight districts of Bihar where it was launched, the devolution of power to the grass roots level remind a misnomer. This study holds that the gap between theory and practice continued to remain. However, there are some striking points of the Panchayati Raj system in Bihar which the author refers to that the Panchayat is a training ground at the grass roots level which provides an opportunity for the transformation of local leadership into district and state level leadership. The Panchayat remained an institution led by local bureaucracy, and hence to self-dependence and self-reliance among the rural masses could not develop. And without the necessary financial backing the Panchayat remained hollow in its functions. The attitude of the state government towards the Panchayati Raj Institutions remained generally indifferent.

Desai (1990)[33] deals with a Responsive Administration in Rural areas for their Integrated development, contains source readings about Panchayati Raj and its problems. Thus, the study of Panchayati Raj has been analyzed in its historical perspective. An attention is also given to social and economic thought which other surveys, concentrating on political thought, have generally omitted. He studies systematically the varied issues of Panchayati Raj and its administration which will provide the necessary momentum to development in India and pleads for accelerated development of rural areas which is essential for a balanced growth of Indian Economy. He also emphasized the importance of Panchayati Raj in the implementation of multi-directional programmes in rural development. He analyses the relevant problems of functions, finances, management and the organisation of programmes initiated to improve the living conditions of the rural people. He contains relevant suggestions and management for speedy rural development.

Murthy (1969)[34] found that if the Sarpanch, who holds a key position in executing the schemes for Scheduled Castes and Scheduled Tribes, is directly elected by the people and not indirectly by the members of the panchayat, then the interests of scheduled castes and scheduled tribes can be secured better. He has made another important observation with regard to the utilisation of resources: the specific funds allotted for the amelioration of SCs and STs under the jurisdiction of Panchayat Samitis have usually been merged with other funds and directed for different purposes.

Parvathamma (1975)[35] analyzed the Impact of PRI on Weaker Sections. One of her observations is that political representation has not helped to bring about the desired level of development among the SCs. She contends that there are built-in drawbacks which prevent the people of these categories from becoming vocal and assertive and much less to mobilise. To quote her "Poverty, ignorance, illiteracy, the near total dependence on upper castes and above all the lowest ritual rank which makes them a constant source of pollution to caste Hindus certainly limits the scope of the roles they could play as panchayat members.

Ali's (1964)[36] report points out that by and large, the PRI have not been able to devote any special attention and render any significant help to weaker sections mostly due to limited financial resources. Under the existing circumstances and limitations, "PRIs have not exhibited any special solicitude for the welfare of the weaker sections of the community."

Gurumurthy (1987)[37] pointed out that the Participation of Weaker Sections as Panchayati Raj Functionaries at the village level is not satisfactory. They continued to be passive participants in its meetings and proceedings. This is because they lacked the essential requisites of participation like education and sufficient income.

Adiseshaiah (1964)[38] observed that the Involvement of Pradhans in the Implementation of Schemes has given Scope for Corruption. As a result, the actual beneficiaries do not get their due and only those beneficiaries who aligned with the pradhans receive some benefits. Even schemes, which were meant for the SCs are manipulated in favour of those who are close to the pradhans. The most deserving cases remained deprived of the benefits of such development schemes. This became possible because of the in-built scope for manipulations at different levels. The well-to-do pradhans had the capabilities and; resources for carrying out such manipulations.

Shymala (2001)[39] conducted study on 594 Zilla Panchayat Members in Karnataka, of which 232 were females and 362 males. Specific purpose of the study was to know (a) socio-economic, political and cultural background of the members, and (b) their perceptions and aspirations about the working of Panchayats in relation to the expectations of the people and the villagers in general. These are the specific findings:

In case of both males and females the number of Zilla Panchayat members are more than 50 years of age are very small, but in the case of age upto 30 years the number of female members is much higher than the male members. However, maximum members from both the sexes (40%) are from the age group of 31-40 years. Maximum respondents are Hindus but among them are either from the dominant castes (29%) or from the scheduled castes (20%). The number of illiterates is much lower (1.34%) but the number of graduates and above, in the case of both the sexes, is much higher (33%). About 5 percent members are wage earners and 70 percent are the cultivators. The members are from the land owner families. While about 7 percent are from the landless category, about 36 percent members own more than 10 acres of land. But about 38 percent members are from below the poverty line.

Large number of members (68%) have political experience, but disparity exists in terms of sex because in contrast to 82 percent males only 47 percent females have that experience. Social service, welfare of the weaker sections etc. were the main motive behind entering the PRI. The respondents received help of both formal and informal sources to win the election. However, formal sources were more important than the informal. So far as development work is concerned, most of them (48% and 36%) have concentrated on welfare and infrastructural development activities respectively. Although 70 percent come from farming background, only 9 percent representatives have done work exclusively for agricultural development. However, the author did not give explanation to this phenomenon. Further, no effort was made to test the validity of the responses pertaining to performance of the respondents as shared by them.

In other study, Aziz (1994)[40] found more or less the same phenomena. While dealing with the Relationship Between local level Traditional Power Structure, Panchayati Raj and the Dalits he said, "attempt made to access power to weaker sections by reserving seats and executive positions have altered hitherto dominant caste centred rural power structure. It should now go to the credit of the makers of law to have given seats and executive positions to the extent of 18 percent to SC and ST candidates and 33.3 percent each to backward communities and women. However, since most of the elected representatives are first generation politicians there is a need for providing training to them" (pp. 132-47).

Singh (1985)[41] observed that in the case of U.P. most of the rural leaders of scheduled castes are now young and literate and hail from dominant caste and well to do families amongst their caste groups. Their exposure to mass media, political awareness and political participation is on the increase, but it cannot be rated as very high or satisfactory, which may be the consequences of their socio-economic backwardness. Their entry to the power and authority structure is by and large moved through the process of reservations. But it would be wrong to say that they cannot share power otherwise. Some of them are emerging as leaders by contesting unreserved seats also. This reflects that they are fitting into the larger political processes in the body politics. But their emergence as successful leaders depends upon the group support structure they have. Generally only those persons are able to emerge as leaders who have strong caste, kin and village factional bases. From the point of view of social values they stand half-way between tradition and modernity; they are highly development oriented but feel helpless and are not able to do much because of the oppressive attitudes of the higher castes and classes. Again they are quite responsive to the people of SCs but feel dissatisfied with the role and attitude of the leaders of their own castes and communities. On the whole the findings lend credence to the hypothesis that instead of continuing the old and traditional, the leadership emerging among SCs is new and development oriented and mobility oriented and large sections of them belong to landless working class.

Kanango (1996)[42] discusses Women's leadership in the Panchayati Raj with special reference to the state of West Bengal. The main purpose of this paper is to examine women's leadership in the political arena in the background of the 73rd Constitutional amendment. The author observed that all women candidates were not necessarily formal members of political parties. Different parties identified some female relations of male members and nominated them. Another factor for selecting women candidates is their background and training in different areas. For example, quite a few *Anganwadi* workers got nomination and got elected too. It was also seen that women instructors of Adult Literacy Centres were selected for nomination. Besides, many of the women candidates had undergone a number of training under TRYSEM, DWCRA and some other programmes carried out by the Development Block.

Women entered in Panchayat politics for various reasons. Some entered because they were asked by the party, but some entered in order to get high status. Women representatives also face difficulties. One of the representatives said, "Spoke in the meetings about the needs of my area. Had been attending the meetings quite regularly in the beginning but the men folks do not pay any attention to what I say, do not give any importance. What is the point in attending meetings when I cannot do anything for the people of my area? So I have stopped attending the panchayat meetings since the last six months."

Socio-cultural factors are also acting as a deterrent in many cases. For example, at night if any emergency arises, women obviously are not allowed to go to the spot and help. Even during the day many families object to their going out to settle any dispute among the villagers. Rather their husbands are made to do the job. Apart from attending official meetings at the panchayat or *Panchayat-Samiti* parents'/in-laws'/husband's permission is necessary to visit any other place.

The author concluded that besides various socio-cultural deterrent the effective participation of women in panchayat may be increased provided they attend training programme on regular basis, mindset of all the political parties are made favourable to them and women's organisations put constant pressure on society for its favour.

Pai (1998)[43] studied the Functioning of *Pradhans* in the Villages in the District of Meerut in Western U.P. All the Panchayat representatives were dalit. She found that reservation alone cannot change the status of women in the family and society and thereby ensure their participation in local bodies. The study also shows that rise in family income and improved lifestyle due to better educational qualification, or investment in business by the male members does not make a difference. The position of women and the perception that they have little knowledge about politics and are incapable of taking part in public affairs, even of independent voting, remain strong. The *Pradhanis* in sampled villagers are mere name sake representatives for the male members of their households. The author added that economic development due to green revolution and market economy has improved income of the sampled households tremendously but have introduced little changes in the social status of women members. On being questioned, all the *Pradhans* said they had agreed to stand for election due to family pressure and the decision of their community, and not because they were keen to do so. All the *Pradhans* were illiterates and only able to put their signatures on official papers. All of them looked upon the Panchayat as a government organisation run by officials and participation by the villagers was seen as unnecessary. Finally, Pai suggested that in order to empower these representatives there is, besides reservation, need a develop not only participatory mechanism of empowerment, but also the means to overcome the structural inequalities of social power. However, without promoting female literacy, independent voting rights, improvement in their status within the family, their proper participation in public sphere may not be ensured.

Mahipal (1998)[44] studied the Problems of 651 Women Panchayat Representatives of all the Levels. These women were from U.P. Most of these representatives were dalit, illiterate and poor. He could narrate twelve problems narrated by these women. These were the following:

(a) majority of respondents are not informed about the schemes and the proposed meetings at the Block level. Even if they are informed, in most of the cases they are not allowed by the male family members to attend it. One of the respondents said that "They once went to the Block office to cast their votes in the election of the *Pramukh.* Except that they do not know what role they have in PRIs."

(b) they added that for economic purpose they have to depend on their husbands,

(c) due to fear of above they do not allow girls to attend schools located outside the village,

(d) they are denied *Patta of* their land which they are cultivating since long,

(e) malfunctioning of the PHCs or its poor management,

(f) no improvement in drainage and drinking water facility,

(g) malfunctioning/favouritism in public distribution system shop,

(h) lack of toilet and other essential facility at the place of meeting at Block office,

(i) no-confidence motions against women *Pradhans* are moved in number of GPs. As a result functioning of GP has been affected, GP is failed to mobilises its own resources because as soon as it imposes taxes, it is opposed by the villagers.

It was found that bureaucracy was not cooperative in empowering the women. It feels superior to the elected representatives of the panchayats. To quote the author.

Buch, Jain and Chaudhary (1999)[45] conducted Study on Women in Panchayati Raj in Madhya Pradesh. The study was conducted in three district socio-cultural zones where the ST, SC was others are numerically dominant. So far as their socio-profile is concerned, the study documented that maximum number of PRI leaders (307 out of 343) are from the marginalised groups. 283 women and 80 men participated in the study. Majority of the leaders are above the age of 25 years 'they are engaged in agricultural work'. In fact, either they are the wage earners or cultivators. Although, there is slight district-wise variation but majority of the respondents are from below the poverty line. More than 50 percent are illiterate. Even in the case of chairpersons out of 72, 23 are illiterate. Most of them had no affiliation with any of the political parties in the formal sense. 53 respondents are landless but a good number of them (126) possess either or more than 5 acres of land. It is interesting to note that a good number of respondents have discontinued labour work after becoming PRI leaders but even today 92 are engaged. This work of the study concluded that PRI is numerically imitated by the leaders of lower socio-economic status in M.P.

Nayak (1996)[46] studied the Nature and Extent of Violence against the Panchayat Representative of Dalit community. Citing the case of stripping of Draupadi Bai, a Dalit Sarpanch of Rajgarh district (M.P.) before the BDO on November 19, 1995 the author mentioned that during 1994 election she along with three other women contested the election. The panchayat was reserved for ST women. She defeated the contestants who were Congress supporters. Draupadi is literate, 50 years old poor woman. M. Agarawal (42) was one of the immigrants inhabitants in the village. He belonged to the rich family, but he was a dull man. He had extramarital relation with Bunda Bai (ST). He wanted to get Bunda elected as *Sarpanch* so as to control the Panchayat fund. But it did not materialised. She was defeated. From the date of defeat of Bunda onward Agarwal begins to search opportunity to humiliate Draupadi. In the meantime he succeeded in getting a contract to construct a school building with the help of a non-tribal Panch. He made allegation of misuse of fund against Draupadi. No-confidence motion was brought against her. In that meeting she was badly humiliated/ abused even before the pressure of BDO and other officials. At 2 a.m. she tried to escape from the meeting but Agarwal and others pulled her *Sari* and she felled.

Datta (1997)[47] studied the Nature of Relationship between the Established Upper Caste Leadership and the Emerging *Dalit* leadership in Panchayat. He is of the view that in spite of prolonged backwardness and economic dependence, the poor Dalits may replace the rich leadership of the upper castes, if they are united, assertive and dedicated. The victory of Maiah Wankhede (SC woman) as sarpanch prove this proposition. She herself is an upper caste, educated and urban based woman. But she got married with a dalit activist. When she heard that the panchayat was reserved for women candidates, she decided to contest the election. But the opponent was from a well-to-do family, the family which had dominated the local politics since last 30 years. In spite of all ethical, and non-ethical means adopted by the powerful opponent, she won the election only because (a) she and her panel promised the villagers that it will solve the problem of water, toilet and fuel which is faced by the majority, (b) they wrote slogans on walls of each of the houses in the village. In fact not a single wall was left for the opposition to write on. The opposition adopted different techniques. They used and manipulated family pressure, money, liquor, political institution and traditions to win the battle. But they did not succeed.

Similar observation was made by Lele (2001).[48] In course of the Comparative Study Between Traditional Village Panchayat and the modern *Gram Sabha* in Maharashtra from the point of view of empowerment of the weaker sections, the author opined that of course platform of statutory *Gram Sabha* is theoretically opened for the marginalised but in the real sense it is not. In fact, alienation from the political processes seems to prevail and that is why even reservation has not helped to make the marginalised more vocal. This then creates the right conditions for the domination of traditional power of the upper castes and classes. The other factor is economic dependence of the marginalised on the dominants. For those who work on the fields or run small shops or are service providers, opposing the *gavki* is unthinkable. They would be digging their own graves by opposing the upper castes and rich farmers on whose fields they work and earn their daily wages. Besides, personal loans are also made available by the same people, those who constitute the *gavki*. Thus, opposing the *gavki* could mean starvation as a result of boycott by the rich peasants and others (p. 4703).

Pundir (1995)[49] conducted a study in four areas located in eastern and western parts of UP to know (a) to what extent the scheduled castes have been participating in the political process? and (b) whether this participation is leading to participation in decision making? The four areas where the study was conducted are different to each other from the point of view of socio-economic conditions of the dalits. For example, in situation 'a' the scheduled caste is numerically superior, they are occupationally diversified and economically independent. They are a bit modernised. In situation 'b' they are more than 20 percent population and neither high nor low. In the situation 'c' the SC is politically developed. They organise and consolidate the other scheduled castes for their common cause. The situation 'd' is from the eastern U.P. Here the dalits only participate in voting. There is very less degree of organisation of the scheduled castes even for their own affairs. In response to the above two questions the following scenario emerged:

1. The scheduled caste is participating in the political processes to a large extent at the local level and has achieved positions of members, somewhere also the highest power position. As members, largely they go on the basis of reservation of seats and also on general seats exceptionally.

2. The SC members and the highest position holders participate in the decision-making to a large extent and influence to some extent, also influence in their favour. This is also generating self-confidence and efficacy among them to some extent. But the extent of this decision-making and efficacious participation is not the same in all the above four situations. Actually where there is numerical superiority of SC population and they are economically and occupationally independent, in that situation the extent and nature of political participation is excellent. The numerical strength alone is not sufficient. Since in the situation 'd' there is almost lack of social capital the level of participation is low. Hence, conclusion of Pundir is more or less similar to the conclusion of Pai.

Research Gap

Studies on political participation of weaker sections have acquired a great social science significance and political significance. Many political scientists, sociologists, anthropologist have studies different, tribes, castes, communities and their leaders. There were studies with special reference to their problems and the role of government in implementing social welfare programmes and to achieve social justice. The foregoing literature clears highlights a despite gap. Thus, the present study is to fill up gap between theory and practice. Since advocate numbers of representatives belonging to OBC are working in Panchayat Raj Institutions, due to the provisions of 73rd Constitutional Amendment Act. And as per the constitutional provisions a number of welfare schemes/ programmes are being implemented thorough the PRI in Karnataka.

All these studies contributed to identify the different aspects of PRIs in India, but not directly focused on the nature of social categories among BCs and factors influencing them to capture various positions in PRIs reserved in the name of BCs. Thus, the present study is one of the interdisciplinary one and has national and international relevance. And in view of this, all these literature which was reviewed facilitates the researcher to adopt appropriate methodology, to prepare to relevant objectives, hypotheses, tools for collecting data, interpretation, analysis and to find out the findings with suitable recommendations.

Interdisciplinary Relevance

In Andhra Pradesh the total number of Gram Panchayats (21913), Mandal Panchayats (1096), Zilla Panchayats (22) Members in Gram Panchayats : GM - 160386, SC – 31243, ST - 16662, Women - 68736 (Total – 208291) Members in Mandal Panchayats : GM - 10938, SC – 2586, ST -1093, Women - 4919 (Total – 14617) Members in Zilla Panchayats : GM - 812, SC – 196, ST - 87, Women - 364 (Total – 1095).

As per the panchayat act of 1995, 33% of seats have been reserved for BCs and the political process of these sections have changed the social conditions to some extend in some parts of Andhra Pradesh. However, the reservation provisions are not being utilised by the people with less agrarian resources and low social status. Therefore, the present study intends to examine the nature of social categories occupying the positions in PRIs among BCs. And pros and cons of reservation provision on BCs in different areas of Andhra Pradesh. Thus, the present study has its interdisciplinary relevance as the study is identifying social, economic, cultural and educational factors influencing on the working of BCs in PRIs in relation to caste and faction dominated society.

Significance of the Study

The study had a vast significant interims of understanding the political process of Backward Castes (BCs) in Panchayat raj

Institutions and its pros and cons in the state of Andhra Pradesh, where the agrarian structure, economic sources are being controlled by major communities. As these major land owning communities and other occupants of important positions of villages traditionally controlling the village politics for centuries. The purpose of the study is to understand the impact of reservation provisions for BCs in PRIs and the role of BCs in achieving the welfare of BCs in a caste dominated society. There are three categories of social groups resulted by rituals, economy and occupation. As a result of traditional occupation the lower social group was formed, because they are engaging in less income activities and living in chronic poverty. They are backward in terms of educationally, socially, economically and culturally. Under the circumstances the present study has its relevance to assess the nature of BCs with in categories are working in PRIs in Andhra Pradesh. It is also intended to examine whether the reservation provisions of 73rd amendment act really utilised by appropriate or genuine social groups among BCs in the state of Andhra Pradesh. It is to assess whether the positions in PRIs are captured by agrarian, economically dominated groups among BCs. The study is also intends to examine the role of caste and its dominance in political process of BCS in general and in the institutions of panchayat raj in particular. The focus of the study is to assess the conditions of BC's representatives in issues relating to faction, crime, economic conditions and related issues after 1994. Besides, its attempt to examine the merits and demerits of panchayat raj acts in terms of extending reservation provisions to people belonging to BCs along with policy implications.

The above-mentioned studies have their relevance as well as importance, based on the objectives and type of research work they carried out. Besides all these studies, the present study is entirely different from the other studies as it is taken up in order to examine the nature of representatives among BCs are capturing positions of PRIs, in respect objectives, scope and methodology employed in the present study. Hence, the present study is one of the interdisciplinary one and has national and international status.

Objectives of the Study

The study has the following objectives:[50]

- To assess the representation of backward castes in the institutions of PRIs in relation to social background in the three regions of Andhra Pradesh.
- To examine the welfare of backward categories with the political participation of representatives belonging to backward categories across the regions of Andhra Pradesh.
- To examine the pros and cons of reservation provisions to backward categories after 73rd amendment act in the three regions of Andhra Pradesh.
- To examine the factors determining for the involvement of BCS in PRIs in the three regions of Andhra Pradesh.
- To assess the role of caste, social status and agrarian resources to capture various positions in institutions of Panchayat raj in the three regions of Andhra Pradesh.
- It is to assess the response of dominant castes towards the representatives of backward castes in the three regions of Andhra Pradesh.
- To examine the nature of political process of backward categories among the BCs through the PRIs.
- To assess the economic, crime and faction status of the families of representatives of BCs in PRIs in districts of Rayalaseema.
- To examine whether people belonging to higher social categories within backward castes are capturing the positions in PRIs or low social categories.

- To find out the reasons why the people belonging to lower social categories among Backward castes are not capturing the various positions in PRIs across the regions of Andhra Pradesh
- To recommend policy implications for achieving social justice by providing opportunities to the people belonging to lower social and economic categories in the three regions of AP.

Hypotheses

The study have the following Hypotheses: [51]

- The reservation benefits in PRIs has reached only the dominant social categories among the BCs in Andhra Pradesh.
- The representatives belonging to BCs in panchayat raj institutions in the three regions of Andhra Pradesh are being controlled by upper caste people.
- The developmental programmes in PRIs are being utilised by the people belonging to higher economic groups among BCs.
- In Rayalaseema region representatives from BCs are involving in factions in the process of political participation and for their survival.
- The reservation benefits of 73rd amendment act have not reached to people belonging to lower castes among BCs.

Methodology

The aim of the study is to assess the status of backward castes with reference to the nature of social categories among the BCs. The important focus of the study is to identify the factors affecting the really backward categories in political process in the institutions of panchayat raj. The aim of the study is also to assess the impact of social status (caste) in the political process of BCs in particular and in the working of PRIs in general. The study is to examine the social, economic and crime status of families of representatives in PRIs in regions of Rayalaseema. As the study intends to examine which categories from BCs are capturing the positions in PRIs by the reservation provisions and finally to evaluate the over all benefits of welfare policies whether reached to the needy people from BCs or not. For this purpose an Analytical, Descriptive and Normative methods have been employed in the study.[52]

Research Design

As the study is to be conducted in the three regions of Andhra Pradesh and the purpose of the study is to find out whether the positions in PRIs are being captured by higher social categories with better agrarian resources among BCs after 73rd amendment act. It is to suggest the policy implications for the political participation of lower strata categories among BCs in PRIs in the three regions of Andhra Pradesh. For this purpose the required data for the present study has been conducted randomly with the help of stratified random technique. The proposed study was conduced in the three regions of Andhra Pradesh viz., Telangana, Andhra and Rayalaseema, two mandals from each district were chosen taking in to consideration of literacy, unemployment, nature of caste among BCs and their population, social and development indicators in-depth analysis of representation of BCs was made. The factors affecting for non-involvement of people from lower social categories among BCs in the institutions of panchayat raj were also examined. For suggesting policy implications opinions were elicited from the different sections of people using scientific research techniques in the three regions of Andhra Pradesh.

Sourcess of Data

In order to conduct the proposed study the required information will be conducted from both primary and secondary sources. The macro aspect of the study will be based on the published and unpublished works on the subject, reports of panchayat raj institutions along with government. Exclusively in this study records, reports, annual action plans, budgetary documents, schemes of zilla panchayats and Mandal Panchayats prepared in different districts, district statistics, documents of PRIs in deferent districts were the main sources of data. The uses of websites such as www.ap.nic.in, Andhra Pradesh .com, localgovernmentindia.org, censusindia.com and other leafleted web services were also be used for collecting primary and secondary data. Secondary data was also collected from books, journal and newspapers. In addition to these sources, primary information has been collected through interview scheduled intended to serve to a cross-sections of representatives, officials, caste leads from BCs were used for analysis. The collected primary is 450 in total, which represents 150 from each study area i.e., 150 from Anantapur district, 150 from Warangal district and 150 from East Godawari district.

Techniques of Data Collection and Analysis

In view of the objectives, need and importance of the present study, the required data has been collected using different methods of scientific techniques. Particularly, different methods of social enquiry were adopted. A special tool (questionnaire) was used by the investigator using the scientific process. The questionnaire consists of items in all spread over behaviour areas and also to collect the personal data i.e., name, sex, age, social, economic, political and educational background. Further, the collected data has been analyzed with the help of computer. It was transformed in to computer code and analysis was made with the help of single variable or multivariable tables. Statistical tools such as average, percentage, mean, correlation, cross-sectional and SES has been measured.

Chapterisation

The present study is broadly divided into seven chapters:

The first chapter is introduction, which deals with political participation in general and the participation of backward castes in panchayat raj institutions in India, need and importance of the study, objectives, hypothesis of the study, methodology, sources, data collection and interpretation of the study.

The second chapter deals with evolution of panchayat raj institutions in India, evolution of panchayat raj system in ancient India, villages of ancient India, medieval India, Balwant Ray Mehta Committee report and Ashok Mehta Committee report etc.

The third chapter discusses the panchayat raj system in Andhra Pradesh, structure of panchayat raj system, powers and functions of Zilla Praja Parishad, Mandal Praja Parishad.

The fourth chapter highlights the profile of Andhra Pradesh, demography, literature, rainfall and profiles of study areas i.e., Anantapur, Warangal and West Godavari districts and working of panchayat raj institutions in Andhra Pradesh.

The fifth chapter discusses the socio-economic background of the respondents.

The sixth chapter highlights the perception and problems of political participation of backward castes in Andhra Pradesh.

The last and seventh chapter is conclusion, which focuses on the findings of the study and the policy implications related to the present study.

References

1. Singh, S.N., *Reservation Policy for Backward Classes*, Rawat Publications, Jaipur, New Delhi, 1996, p. 28.
2. Rajesh Kumar, Political Empowerment of Weaker sections: A Study of Municipal Bodies in Haryana, *The Indian Journal of Political Science*, Vol. LXII, No. 3. July – Sep., 2006, p. 457.

3. Syamala Devi, D. and Lakshmi, G., Political Empowerment of Women in Indian Legislature: A study, the *Indian Journal of Political Science,* Vol. LXVI, No. 1, Jan-March, 2005, p. 77.
4. Bajpa, Ashok and Varma, M.S., Panchayat Raj in India" A New Thrust, Sahitya Prakashan, Delhi, 1995, pp. 47-48.
5. 73rd Constitutional Amendment Act, Government of India, 1992, pp. 148.
6. See for details, R.S. Sharma, *Shudras in Ancient India,* Motilal Banarsidas, New Delhi, 1980 and D.D. Kosambi, *An introduction to the study of Indian history,* Popular Prakashan, Bombay, 1975.
7. Gail Omvedt, *Dalits and Democratic Revolution,* Sage Publications, New Delhi.
8. Javeed Alam, *Is Caste Appeal Casteism? Oppressed Castes in Politics,* Economic and Political Weekly, March 27, 1999, Vol. xxxiv, No. 13, p. 757.
9. Nomita Yadav, *Other Backward Classes: Then and Now,* Economic and Political Weekly, November 2-9, 2002, Vol. xxxvii, Nos. 44 and 45, p. 4495.
10. Caste, Class and Social Articulation in Andhra Pradesh, India: Mapping Differential Regional Trajectories, Overseas Development Institute, 01-Nov-2002, p. 27.
11. Barbara C Burrel, *Women and Political participation,* Library Congress Cataloging - in - Publication, USA, 2004. p. 43.
12. Sam Peltzman, *Political Participation and Government Regulations,* The University of Chicago Press, 1998. p. 39.
13. Mishra, Swetha, *Democratic Decentralisation in India.* Mittal Publications, New Delhi, 1989.
14. Verma, S.L., "State Autonomy and Democratic Decentralisation" (Ed.) and *Panchayat Raj Grama Swaraj and Federal Polity,* Rawat Publications, Jaipur, Edition: 1990, pp. 125-129.
15. Nagendra Ambedkar, *New Panchayat Raj at work,* ABD Publishers, Jaipur, India, 2000.
16. Malviya, H.D. Village Panchayats in India, All India Congress Committee, New Delhi, 1956.
17. Maddick, Henry, *Panchayat Raj: A study of Rural Local Government in India,* Longman, London, 1970.
18. Asha Koushik, "Constitutionalisation of Panchayat Raj in the Gandhain Perspective: Ed. R.P. Joshi, *Constitutionalisation of Panchayat Raj,* Rawat Publications, Jaipur, 1998.

19. Sammiuddin Abida, A critique of Panchayat Raj with Special Reference to Uttar Pradesh, Sahitya Bhavan Agra, 1976.
20. Laxmi Narayan, H.D., *India's Villages at Gross roots* National Publishing House, New Delhi, 1976.
21. Narayan, E.A. "Panchayat Raj and Scheduled Castes, Scheduled Tribes and Other Backward Class". Edited by R.P. Joshi, *Constitutionalisation of Panchayat Raj*, Rawat publications, Jaipur, 1998.
22. Gehlot, N.S., "Towards Panchayat Raj: Some Myths of Democratic", Edited in R.P. Joshi, *Constitutionalisation of Panchayat Raj*, Rawat Publication, Jaipur, 1998.
23. Rao, D.V. Raghava, *Panchayats and Rural Development*, Ashish Publishing House, New Delhi, 1980.
24. Report of the Committee to Review the Existing Administrative Arrangement of Rural Developments and Poverty Alleviation Programmes (CAARD), Govt. of India, New Delhi, 1985.
25. Planning Commission, *First Five Year Plan,* New Delhi, 1952, p. 223.
26. Prasad, R.C., *Democracy and Development: The Grass Roots Experience in India*, Rachana Prakashan, New Delhi, 1971.
27. Kumar, Sushil and K. Venkataraman, *State Panchayati Raj Relations: A Study of Supervision and Control in Tamil Nadu*, Asia Publishing House, Bombay, 1974.
28. Pant, Niranjan, *The Politics of Panchayati Raj Administration: A Study of Official and Non-official Relations,* Concept Publishing Co., Delhi, 1979.
29. Darshankar, Arjun, Y., *Leadership in Panchayati Raj: A Study of Beed District of Maharashtra,* Panchsheel Prakashan, Jaipur, 1979.
30. Sharma, Surjit Singh, *Rural Elites in India,* Sterling Publishers Pvt. Ltd., New Delhi, 1979.
31. Bhargava, B.S., *Panchayati Raj System and Political Parties,* Ashish Publishing House, New Delhi, 1979.
32. Singh, Rajendra Prasad, *Bihar Men Gram Panchayat,* Bihar Hindi Granth Academy, Patna, 1987.
33. Desai, Vasant, *Panchayati Raj: Power to the People,* Himalaya Publishing House, Bombay, 1990.
34. Murthy, O.K. (1969): Some Reflections on the Duplication of the Panchayati-Raj on the Weaker Sections of the Community, in the Proceedings of the 15th Conference of the K.S. Co.
35. Parvathamma (1975): "Panchayati-Raj and Weaker sections", Presented at the Seminar held in NIRD, Hyderabad (Unpublished paper).

36. Ali, Saliq (1964): Report of the Study Team on Panchayati Raj, Jaipur: Panchayat and Development, Govt. of Rajasthan.
37. Gurumurthy, U., (1987): *Panchayati Raj and Weaker Sections*, New Delhi: Ashish Publishing House, p. 168.
38. Adiseshaiah (1964): Social Background and Role Preferences of Village Pradhans, New Delhi: Institute of Social Sciences, p. 39.
39. Shyamala, C.K. (2001): "Evaluation of Decentralised Governance and Planning in Karnataka", Man and Development, June.
40. Aziz, A. (2000): "Democratic, Decentralisation–Experience of Karnataka", Economic and Political Weekly, Vol. XXXV, No. 39, Sept. 23-29.
41. Singh, D.R. (1985): *Rural Leadership Among Scheduled Castes,* Allahabad: Chugh Publications, pp. 189-202.
42. Kanango, S.D. (1996): "Panchayati-Raj and Emerging Women Leadership: An Overview", Social Action, Vol. 46, January-March.
43. Pai, S. (1998): Pradhanis in New Panchayats: Fields notes from Meerut District", Economic and Political Weekly, Vol. XXIII, No. 18, May 2-8, pp. 1009-10.
44. Mahipal (1998): "Women in Panchayat: Experiences of a Training Camp", Economic and Political Weekly, Vol. XXIII, No.4, Jan.24-30, pp. 150-152.
45. Buch, N., Jain, U. and Chaudhary, S.N. (1999): Women in Panchayati Raj in Madhya Pradesh, (Mimeo) Bhopal: Mahila Chetna Manch.
46. Nayak, R.C. and George Mathew (1996): "Panchayat at Work: What it means for the oppressed?," Economic and Political Weekly, July 6, p. 20.
47. Datta, Bishaka (ed), (1977): "The Amount of Work the Ladies did, the Men will not do and who will make the Chapatis: A study of All-Women Panchayats in Maharashtra", Calcutta; Stree.
48. Lele, M.K. (2001): "Local Government: Conflict of Interests and Issues of Legitimisation", Economic and Political Weekly, Vol. XXXVI, No. 51, Dec. 22-28.
49. Pundir, J.K. (1995): "Development of Scheduled Castes: A Study of their Political and Decisive Participation at Local Level in Rural areas", AJSDJ, Vol. III, pp. 49-64.
50. C.R. Kothari, *Research Methodology: - Methods and Techniques,* New Age International Pvt. Limited, Publishers, New Delhi, 2006. p. 76.
51. C M Recto Branch, Research Methods and Thesis Writing, Manila, 32.
52. Wane Goddard and Stuart Melville, Research Methodology an Introduction, Berne Convention, 2007. p. 9.

Chapter - II

Evolution of Panchayat Raj Institutions in India

This chapter is intended to discuss the Evolution of Panchayati Raj system in ancient India, medieval period and British period. It also considers in short the glimpses of development of Panchayati Raj system after independence.

Evolution of Panchayati Raj System in Ancient India

Panchayati Raj is not a new concept to India. Panchayats have been a part of rural cultural heritage of India. From time immemorial, panchayats have enjoyed the confidence of the people. The system has survived in spite of turmoils and changes, because the village folk were fully confident of their own capabilities of sound thinking and right approach to their problems.

Panchayat literally means an assembly (yat) of five (panch) wise and respected elders chosen and accepted by the village community. They were considered as the incarnation of God (panch parameshwar). Panchayats had a wide spectrum of activities covering executive, administrative, developmental and judiciary. They breathed health in to the rural society.

Villages of Ancient India

The autonomous village is best described by Sir Charles

Metcalf: The village communities are little republics, having nearly everything they can want within themselves. Dynasty after dynast tumbles down; revolutions succeed revolution, but the village community remains the same. This union of village communities, each one forming a separate little state in itself, has contributed more than any other to the cause of the preservation of the people of India and the enjoyment of freedom and independence.[1]

In ancient India people were living in joint families. The patriarch of the joint family wielded very wide powers over its members. A federation of such small families were living in a village. The seniormost member of the seniormost family in the village was regarded with great reverence by the village community and was entrusted with the governmental functions.

The institutions of joint family thus gradually led to the evolution of kingship. Since ancient times, the village has been the unity of administration. Its importance was naturally very great in an age. When the means of communications and transport was slow and raids were frequent. Villages in ancient India were productive and prosperous and as such their importance in a state or kingdom was very significant. Vedic hymns frequently praged for the prosperity of villages. Kings like Bimbasara used to convene a meeting of village headmen to discuss important questions of administrative policy.

Dr. Altekar sums up aptly that, "There is no doubt that villages were the real centres of social life and important units in the country's economy. They sustained the edifice of national culture prosperity and administration".[2]

India has been the cradle of rural local government which continued to flourish from the time of Vedic civilisation to the advent of British rule. In the Indian history the village was the basic unit of Government, whether the central authority was monarchical or republican. The rural local government is the very foundation stone on which every empire in India has been reared. The village in India has been considered as the basic unit of the local self administrations since Vedic times.[3]

The village has been the mainstay of rural India throughout the countries. The term for the village was the "grama" "ksetra" and "usvara" which from rigvedic denoted plough land. The villages were prosperous the Gramik or Gramini and other village elders were responsible for village defence. There was little interference by the state in their activities. The village communities were always self-sufficient, self-reliant and independent.

The village administration was carried on under supervision and direction of the village headmen. Verilly called grama or gramika or grameyaka in northern India, munuda in the eastern deccan, gramukata, or govunda in Karnataka and Mahattaka or Mahantaka in the U.P.

References to such a highly organised system of local government can also be found in the Vedas, in the Epics - of Ramayana and Mahabaratha, Manusmriti, in the literature of Buddhist and Jains and in Koutilya's Arthashastra. The Vedas (Rig Vedas in particular) reveal that prime used to live in small traditional guilds; which where generally controlled and regulated by popular institutions.[4]

The control of the state over the village continued to be mentioned in the later days of the Manusmriti in which the king used to place a company of soldiers, commanded by a trusted official, in the midst of two, five or hundreds of villages. The king was empowered to appoint a lord for each village as well as a lord for ten villages (Deshi).

During the period of Buddhism and Jainism villages were classified according to the size and mode of habitation. The villages were self-sufficient and self-dependent. The village headman was known as Bhojak. His duty was to collect the revenue for the state and to organise the constructive programmes. The Bhojak was selected by the villagers on the basis of local customs and traditions.

During the rule of Mouryan Emperors, the process of village administration underwent some changes. Under Chanakya's rule villages were classified according to the population. The village administration during this period (324-236 BC) was closely linked with agriculture. The size of the village varied from 100 to 500 families. The following officials composed the village administrative staff.

1. The headman (Adyaksha).
2. The accountant (Samkhayaka).
3. The village officials of different grades (Sthanikas).
4. The village countries (Jamgha karika).
5. Veterinary Doctor (Anikartha).
6. Village Medical Officer (Chikitska).
7. Horse trainer (Ashwa Damok).

The above mentioned members of assembly were not elected but they were chosen by a sort of natural selection. The headman was the president of the village assembly and its executive official. He was the leader of the village both for civil purposes and for military operations. The members of assembly were wholly responsible for the service of the community in their respective fields.

During the times of Harsha in the sixth century these panchayats were active. There were panchayats for different occupational ground and one for the village as a whole during the post-Mouryan period from 200 BC to 300 AD. Known as the "Dask period" the village continued to be smallest unit of the administration. The headman assisted by the council of elders, still played a prominent role in village life. The village under the Mouryan period was efficiently organised. The traditional elders found that the system and concepts of programmes of the Vedic age were still dominant, was also a feature of Gupta's rule.

The system did not change under the imperial Guptas, although it underwent certain changes in nomenclature. The district official was known as "Vishayapathi". He was a feudatory Maharaja owing allegiance to the emperor and enjoying autonomy in regard to internal matters. He was advised, by guild presidents, chief scribes and leading persons of locality. The villagers were governed by Gramapati (headman) assisted by the village assemblies. The assembly consisted of entire population of war. The male adults and some times Mahattaras (a body of selected elders). The assembly appointed a number of committees to look after the various aspects of village administration.

The village officers consisted of headman, accountant, watchman, school teacher, priest, supervisor of irrigation works and boundary man. All of them were paid according to the local customs either in the form of a grant of rent free land or share of crop at the harvesting time. The village had its own funds. The inference of police officials of the mining department was permitted in special cases but they were very rare.

Thus, in ancient India rural local government was omni-competent, financially viable, practically autonomous and imbued with a gracious civic spirit. It was frictionless machine and characterised by the high degree of efficiency, impartiality and integrity. The panchas has a sense of dedication to the service of the people who had both a sense of involvement and a feeling of independence.

Medieval India

A new chapter of Indian history and culture begins with the arrival of Muslims in India. The first Muslims who came to India were Arabs who conquered Sindh and Multan in 712 AD. With the passage of time, the much-cherished independence of the village bodies began to diminish during the Muslims; particularly the Mughal rulers ultimately succeeded Hindu Rajas. The earlier districts and villages were put under the charge of the centrally appointed subedars, amatyagars, muquaddams and patvaris. The pattern of village local government however continued practically unaltered, thus keeping up the tradition of continuity of local government till the advent of British Raj.

Hugh Tinker says that, "The Mughals had interfered very little with the ancient customs of village government. They incorporated the village into the administration as a unit for revenue and police purposes only. The state through the headman or muqaddam who was held responsible for the maintenance of law and order and the restriction of their within that area of his authority. The Judicial powers of the village council, the panchayat were considerably curtailed, under the mughals, otherwise the local affairs remained unregulated from above and the village officers and servants were answerable primarily to the panchayats".[5]

Though Muslim rulers did not interfere with the working of local institutions very much, still due to the strict bureaucracy, the cultivators and to suffer very much in closing years of Shah Jahan's rule, in fact, these nobles became more democratised, the peasants were more harassed by the provincial Government, their condition decorated and the evil of pauperism increased.[6]

The villages lost all powers and the village assembly had no influence. There was no direct relationship between the villagers and the state. No attention was paid to the development of local institutions. But Akbar the great, was an exception who reorganised the whole revenue system by establishing direct relations of state with the cultivators. The village headsman that was known as Choudhari, or Mukhiya or Muqaddam, was treated as village servant and responsible for the public works. This muqaddam was the main link between the government and the village. The government dealt with the peasants through him. It may be presumed that the village headman was the most important individual in the general economy of village.

One of the important features of the Mughal rule was the growth of urban centers. In the newly established towns, the development of the local government was more marked. The office of the Kotwal was created and the entire town administration was put under his charge. The rulers were very interested in the development of towns and as a result the village remained largely unaffected.

The Mughal system of administration was regulative, they hardly thought of welfare activities particularly in the villages. Further, the lack of means of communication made it difficult to have close links everywhere in the system of administration. The lack of rapid communication was helpful in eventual survival of local self-governments. It can thus be inferred that the very spirit and form of panchayats during the Mouryan and Gupta periods were present in the Muslim period. There was anarchy or military despotism throughout wide areas of India between the disintegration of the Mughal Empire and the advent of the British Raj.

British Period

With the fall of Mughal Empire, a disorder overtook the country and western traders used this time for their own fortification and establishment. In this period the panchayats continued to function quite vigorously and were fully respected by the then government.

The panchayats were quite strong and active before the English took over the administration of this country. The British rule resulted in a direct attack on the institution of panchayats. The panchayats were ordered not to interfere in the administrative and judicial functions of the state. Then the administrative field was so much extended that every function of the panchayat fell within its jurisdiction. In a short time, the village organisation of autonomous nature in all spheres of life i.e., panchayats also disappeared. In fact, the whole of the old and ancient structure trembled down to the utter misery and poverty of the poor village.

India became a market place for British goods and storage of raw materials for the British industries. Indians were forced now to completely depend upon the foreign markets for most of these bare needs. The authority of the panchas and sarpanchas to deliver justice locally was covertly taken away and was vested in the centrally created imperial courts. The Lambardar was a selected representative from the property holding group. Though the office of the Lambardar was hereditary, in some cases the villagers could remove him. In practice, his office got much power and practically no one dared to oppose or criticize him.

However, a few Presidencies Government still made some attempts here and there to keep these institutions alive. The Charter Act 1793 was the first statutory enactment regulating municipal administration for the presidency towns. Outside the presidency towns the first attempts to introduce municipal government was made through the Bengal Act of 1842, enabling the inhabitants of any locality to make better provisions for public health for which they were asked to pay the taxes levied for the purpose. The Act of 1850 allowed the government to create municipalities into those towns where the inhabitants desired them.

The most remarkable innovation proposed by Lord Rippon in 1882, was the establishment of rural local bodies. It created a two-tier system with district boards and sub-district boards based on either the sub-division or the tahsil. These district boards composed of officials and elected members, and encourage the establishment of active village panchayats. But the innovation did not bear much fruit. It had organisation and control but lacked the vital spirit of democracy. The boards came under the control of district officers of the provinces and the panchayats received only lukewarm support from the Indians themselves. Lack of co-operation in implementation killed the Rippon proposals and the great intentions of the originator remained ineffective for a long time to come.

The main object of the British in India being the exploitation of the country, the panchayats were dissolved and completely suppressed. By the abolition of these institutions there was no institution left through which a strong link between the government and the villages could be established. With such objectives the government appointed a Royal commission in the year 1907 on decentralisation process.

The Commission was presided over by C.E.H. Hobhouse, as its Chairman. The Commission was set-up by the liberal government to inquire into the financial and administrative relations of the government of India and the provincial government and of authorities subordinated to them, to report whether by measure might be simplified and improved.

The committee submitted its report in 1909 and with this a new form of local self-government under the British rule in India began. The report also explored the disappearance of villages long enjoyed. The commission wanted that the panchayats should be kept under a separate department. The report also suggested on average five members with village headman as ex-officio chairman of the panchayats who must be elected by the villagers.

In August 1917, Montague the Secretary of State for India, who enunciated the future policy of the British government, promised the gradual development of self-government institutions for progressive realisation of responsible government in India. The report on the Indian constitutional reforms (1918) remarked, "There should be, as far as possible complete popular control in local and laigest possiblc independence of them of outside control". It also stated that,

"The government of India proposes to direct attention to the development of panchayats".[7]

With the passing of India Act 1919, Local Self-governments were transferred to Indian ministers who were anxious to make the pattern of local governments more effective. A number of acts were passed by the Provincial Legislative Councils between 1921–26. The Panchayat Acts were passed in Assam, Bengal, Madras, Bombay and the Central Provinces. These acts aimed at lowering the franchise at increasing the elected members in local bodies and at passing executive direction into the non-official hands.

The panchayats were re-shaped to make their composition and functioning more democratic. Where the panchayats did not exist at all, effective steps were taken to establish them. In this way, the panchayats came to be recognised as the basic unit of self-government. The vast tracts of land in the village panchayats and the institution itself needed to be radically restructured on the democrative terms.

The overall growth of panchayats till 1935 was not very encouraging. The Government of India Act of 1935 replaced the diarchy system in the provincial government by provincial autonomy. All provinces enacted legislation for further democratisation of local self-governments. But the provisions of the act could not be fully implemented successfully due to diverse concentration towards Second World War, despite this, certain positive developments took place. They include enlargement of functions in larger bodies, abolition of nomination system, widening of franchise, valuable experience of the working for the representative principle as the technique of committee work and law making. During British regime, the glory and autonomy of ancient and medieval panchayats system was lost. No doubt, the British tried to introduce certain western concepts but no serious and whole-hearted attempts were made for improvements and effective decentralisation.

However, due to strong pressure from the national movement for autonomy and independence, half-hearted and superficial attempts were made for the development of local self-governments throughout the struggle for independence. Mahatma Gandhi clearly advocated strengthening of panchayat raj institutions. His views on Grama Swaraj, Poorna Swaraj and Swadeshi movements had the blend of ideal democracy with decentralisation concept. He believed in the supremacy of people and insisted on the people's democracy and sovereignty at the grass roots level.

Rural Development Process

The introduction of Panchayat Raj system as a main instrument for Rural Development in independent India may be attributed to several factors - India's past history, the teachings of Mahatma Gandhi, the Directive Principles of the Constitution, the Five Year Plans with their endorsement of popular participation and the scheme of Community Development introduced in 1952.[8] The Union Government had appointed a Committee under the chairmanship of Balwant Ray Mehta which is popularly known as the team for the study of community projects and National Extensive Service (NES). It had submitted its report in 1957. It had outlined three main findings. They are:[9] (i) The Community Development and National Extensive Service programme had failed to evoke popular initiative; (ii) Local bodies at a level higher than the Panchayat had evinced but little enthusiasm in the Community Development Programme; and (iii) Even the Panchayat had not come into the field of Community Development in any significant way. The Mehta Committee strongly recommended for decentralisation of responsibility and power to two levels of below the State. It recommended "devolution of power to a body which, when created will have enticed the change of all development work within its jurisdiction, the Government reserving to itself the function of guidance, supervision of higher planning and when necessary providing extra finance.[10]

Balwant Ray Metha Committee Report 1957

After independence, India wanted the development of villages. Therefore, planning commission prepared social and economic plans for the whole India. The various purposes of the plans were to remove illiteracy, poverty, backwardness etc, and also to increase the political participation of people at the local level.

In March 1950, planning commission came into existence. 'The planning commission entrusted the panchayats with new responsibilities. Therefore, planning commission launched the community development and national extension service programmes (CDP and NES) on Oct. 2nd 1952 with the 55 community development projects. The CDP has been the biggest rural reconstruction scheme and it was directly connected with the democratic decentralisation. It was a comprehensive programme, touching all aspects of community life. It was a conscious effort to bring about an all round improvement in living standard of rural population. It was really a concept of all sided development, as distinguished from the development of particular aspects of rural life like agriculture, education, health, animal husbandry, Sanitation etc. CDP aimed at solving all the major problems of villages. It was considered as basically and substantially a programme of the people, for the people and by the people.

However, CDP could not make a satisfactory head way. Because people's participation was not coming forth to a desirable extent. Instead of being a people's programme with the assistance of the government, it was becoming more and more a government programme with varying degree of the people's participation. Therefore, Balwant Ray Mehta Study team was appointed on 1957 to study the CD and NES programmes; especially from the point of view of assessing the extent of popular participation. This committee submitted its report in late 1957.

It opinioned that the popular participation in CDPs enlisted through adhoc advisory bodies was not adequate and it also felt that a separate set of institutional arrangement would have to be statutorily created to make the popular participation meaningful and effective. Accordingly the committee observed "Admittedly one of the least successful aspect of the CD and NES as we don't discover or create a representative and democratic institution which will supply the local interest, supervision and care necessary objects conform with the needs and wishes of the locality in rest it with adequate powers and assign to it appropriate finances we shall never be able to evoke local interest and excite local initiative in the field of development".[11]

Thus, it appear, that the committee wanted development work in rural areas' must be looked after by the vigorous democratic institutions; and such bodies were must be statutorily elected and they should have the comprehensive duties and functions with the adequate resources and only then these bodies become an instrument of expression of local peoples in regard to local development. In this connection the committee suggested the democratic decentralisation. In the view of committee decentralisations was a process where by the government divests itself completely of certain duties and responsibilities and devolves them on to some other authority. Further the committee while commenting on decentralisation said - "it is true that devolution of responsibility cannot be complete without a complete devolution of all the control over the necessary resources and admittedly such devolution cannot be completely feasible in any country".[12]

In this way need for the decentralisation and meaningful popular participation was effectively stressed by Mehta study team. Hence, the committee suggested the creation of such institution through which popular participation can be achieved. It is popularly known as Panchayati Raj. It is nothing but a institutional building experiment. In his report, regarding this aspect, Mehta suggested the three tier system of elected and organically linked democratic bodies through out the country through necessary legislation in states and Union Territories (UT), namely Village Panchayat, Panchayat Samiti, and Zilla Parishad. Here the committee wanted the entrustment of all planning and development activities to these bodies. The committee however was not in favour of rigidity as regard to the uniform pattern of Panchayati Raj throughout the country.

Ashok Mehta Committee 1977

The rural developmental programmes being implemented through the Panchayat Raj Institutions. These PRIs were based on the recommendations of Balwant Ray Mehta Committee. During 1965-70 there was the integration in the working of Panchayat raj system. It standard declaring in the position and the working. The reasons and food deficit, internal emergency and the number of certainly sponsored schemes was included for rural development.

In view of the allowed mentioned reasons, the new government which came to power in 1977 appointed a committee leaded by a distinguished public leader i.e., Ashok Mehta. The committee was in review and restore the importance of Panchayat Raj Institutions. Particulars it was to suggest measures to strengthen the Panchayat Raj Institutions. "So as to enable a decentralised system of planning and development to be effective".

The committee submitted its report in 1978, and mentioned that panchayat raj institutions had been weakened due to certain adverse factors. Scholar, the structure of Panchayat Raj om adequate and the Gout support was measure. Therefore, these institutions was capable to perform developmental role effectively in a changing socio-economic environment.

The committee also notice that in have states the Panchayat Raj Institutions were performing there role on account of structural adequately and appropriate state governments support.

For the effective of functioning of Panchayat Raj Institutions, the Ashok Mehta committee suggested the following measures:

1. More genuine and effective devolution of power of Panchayat Raj institutions should talk place.
2. Primary unity in the panchayat raj system should be zilla parishad and not the panchayat samittee, as the zilla panchayat has better leadership and resources to play a saptenational developmental role.
3. The Mandal panchayat with appropriate powers and resources and covering same areas development block and larger are that village panchayat should replace the panchayat samittee and the panchayats has it would be more effective in management of development schemes.
4. Administrative wing of zilla panchayat in particular and also that of mandal panchayat should be suitably staffed appropriates led by well qualified senior civil servant.
5. Below the mandal panchayat this should be village community including substantially weaker sections of people to perform function allocated it by the mandal panchayat.
6. Co-ordination between rural development and urban development was sought municipal bodies should have representation in zilla panchayat and mandal panchayat.
7. Political parties should take part in elections of panchayat raj and participate in its working.

8. For improving the capabilities and reorienting the attitudes of peoples. Representatives as well as of bureaucracy within panchayat raj a mass programme of education and training should be set up in place of existing limited one.

The Karnataka Panchayat Raj Act of 1983

When the Janata Party came to power in the State, the government introduced a bill called Zilla Parishads, Taluka Panchayat Samithis, Mandal Panchayats and Nyaya Panchayats Bill in the State Assembly in August 1983. The Bill was referred to the Joint Select Committee of the state legislature. It received the assent of the President in July 1985.[20] It was formally called as the Karnataka Zilla Parishads, Taluka Panchayat Samithis, Mandal Panchayats and Nyaya Panchayats Act of 1985.

The Karnataka Panchayat Raj experiment had attracted nation-wide attention of people from all walks of life about the new experiment of institution building at the sub-regional level. The curiosity was mainly due to different interpretations given to the experiment. Some people viewed it as a revolutionary change in the Indian political system and an important landmark in the history of its development. The Karnataka experiment puts an end to the administrative state and encourages people' involvement in managing public affairs.[21]

Main features of Panchayat Raj Act of 1983

Three-tier system is contemplated in the Act of 1983. The Mandal Panchayats, Taluka Panchayat Samities and Zilla Parishads exist under the Act.

I. Mandal Panchayats

1. The Mandal Panchayat shall consist of elected members at the rate of one member for every 400 population. 25% of the membership will be reserved for women in

every Mandal Panchayat. Out of women representation, one seat would be reserved for women belonging to Scheduled Castes or Scheduled Tribes.

2. Seats in Mandal Panchayats will be reserved for Scheduled Castes/ Scheduled Tribes in the same proportion as the population of SC/ST in the mandal bears to total population of the mandal not less than 18% of the seats. The Mandal Panchayat will be headed by Pradhana and will have Upa-Pradhana also.
3. A Mandal Panchayat will meet at least once in a month.
4. The function of Mandal Panchayats would be to look after as far as the funds at its disposal, allow all the matters relating to sanitation and health. Public works and amenities, agriculture and animal husbandry, welfare of Scheduled Castes/Scheduled Tribes and Backward Classes and other matters like preparation of development plans. Promotion/improvement of cottage industries, etc.
5. The Mandal Panchayat will have its own fund in which proceeds from taxes imposed by the Mandal Panchayats and other grants and sums received from government to other bodies will be deposited.

II. Taluka Panchayat Samities

1. This body located at Taluka level and shall consist of members of the State legislature representing a part or whole of Taluka and Pradhan of Mandal Panchayats, President of Taluka Agriculture Produce Coop. Marketing Society, President of Primary Land Development Bank, and 5 members belonging to Scheduled Castes/Scheduled Tribes and backward classes and women opted by resolution of the Taluka Panchayat Samiti, provide not less than 18 percent of the member shall belong to the scheduled castes and scheduled tribes.

2. This body will be headed by Chairman who is Member of Legislative Assembly.

III. Zilla Parishads

1. For each district there shall be a Zilla Parishad.
2. Each Zilla Parishad shall consist of elected members from the talukas in the district. The reservations for Scheduled Castes/Scheduled Tribes will not be less than 18% of the total number of seats in Zilla Parishad and for women 25%. Every Zilla Parishad will have Adhyaksha and Upa-Adhyaksha. Both elected from the members of Zilla Parishads. The Adhyaksha would be executive head of Zilla Parishad.
3. The function of Zilla Parishad would be to oversee the development programmes as well as various sectoral programmes like agriculture, animal husbandry, communication, public health, irrigation, industries, fisheries, etc., as well as welfare of Scheduled Castes/ Scheduled Tribes and Backward Classes.
4. They will formulate and execute the district plans.
5. They shall operate the Zilla Parishad fund, which will be formed from funds transferred to Zilla Parishad out of the Consolidated Fund of State. Grants, fees and penalties, rents from lands, interests, etc.
6. The state government will constitute a Finance Commission consisting of a Chairman and two other members which shall see into the problems of income and expenditure in respect of the Zilla Parishad and recommend to the government as to the pattern of assistance, principles governing the grants-in-aid etc.

IV. Nyaya Panchayats

1. A Nyaya Panchayat shall consist of 5 members elected in accordance with the system of proportional

representation by a single transferable vote by conduct, of which the Mandal Panchayats at least one member shall be each from women, Scheduled Castes/Scheduled Tribes and Backward classes.

2. The Mukhya Nyaya vicharaka shall preside over sitting of Nyaya Panchayat and will be assisted by Secretary of the Mandal Panchayat in performance of its functions.[22]

G.V.K. Rao Committee (1985) (CAARD)

(Committee on Administrative Arrangements for Rural Development)

Therefore the planning commission and the Government of India appointed a committee under the chairmanship of G.V.K. Rao in March 1985, to review the existing administrative arrangements for rural development, poverty alleviation programmes and to recommend appropriate structural mechanism to ensure that these are planned in an integrated manner and effective implementation.

This important recommendations of the committee for as concerned to panchayati raj system are:

The committee observed that, the inadequate resources, irregular elections were the main reason of the failure of the panchayati raj institutions. The committee was of the view that, prime minister would also request to all the chief ministers to hold the regular elections to the panchayati raj institutions whenever due, to give them administrative powers and financial back up to made them popular participation in the development process.

The committee felt that democratically elected local level bodies become responsible to the people there will be effective and meaningful participation of the people in the planning and implementation process. Therefore, Rao committee suggested the regular elections for these institutions.

Rao committee knew that Government machinery (Bureaucracy) alone could not be assigned the responsibility for achieving economic development and social justice, therefore committee in favour of entrusting functions to encompass all social and economic development activities to the different agencies at the field level. The committee considered the panchayati raj institutions as a effective agencies of rural development, here the committee clearly stated that "the fight against poverty can be meaningful only in terms of many sided and total policy thrust and intervention to replace exploitative in egalitarian and oppressive system by a new system oriented to the needs of the poor in key sectors, both on a short term and long term basis".[13]

According to the committee, Zilla Parishad was to be work with the help of the number of departments. Accordingly, the committee proposed the participatory democracy by giving the participative opportunity to the members of the zilla parishad as a member of the one or other committee. Members of the committee's were to be elected by the members of zilla parishad from among themselves on the basis of proportional representation by means of a single transferable vote. The committee suggested the following committees of the Zilla Parishad:

- *Finance standing committee:* It look after the finance, framing of budget, considering proposals for increase in revenue, consideration of proposals affecting finances, examination of receipts and expenditure, internal audit.
- *General standing committee:* It was to look after establishment and miscellaneous residuary matters.
- *Planning committee:* It was to be look after the integrated planning.
- *Antipoverty programme committee:* It was to be responsible for the programmes of IRDP, NREP, RLEGP etc.

- *Public works and Amenities committee:* It was to be concerned to the minor irrigation, district and rural roads, buildings, rural housing, village extensions, rural water supply etc.
- *Agricultural and animal husbandry committee:* It was to look after the agriculture, soil and water conservation, agriculture extension, dry land development, command area development, horticulture etc.
- *Education committee:* It was to be responsible for to look after primary and adults education except academic matters.
- *Health committee:* It was to look after the hospitals, dispensaries, nutrition, rural health and sanitation, rural water supply and family welfare schemes.
- *Industries committee:* It was suggested for the small scale, village and cottage industries, promotion, training, provision of inputs and marketing.
- *Social forestry committee:* It looks after programmes of forestry, minimum needs programmes of rural domestic cooking energy.
- *Social justice committee:* It was concerned to the institutions and programmes for the welfare of SC, ST, Social and women welfare and schemes for other weaker sections of society.

At the lower level the committee, suggested the two different models for the consideration of the state government. One was panchayat samiti another one was mandal panchayat.

L.M. Singhvi Committee

In 1986, the Rajiv Gandhi the then prime minister of India to appoint a committee under the chairmanship of L.M. Singhvi. The committee was to measures for extending the constitutional status to panchayat raj institutions.

The committee enquired about the reasons responsible for the decline of panchayati raj institutions, the committee felt that, lack of conceptual clarity, absence of political will, denial of national priority, lack of continuous process of research, evaluation and feedback were responsible for the decline of panchayati raj institutions.

In the view of the committee panchayati raj institutions are basic unit of self-government and gram sabha as the embodiment of directed to achieve community and social mobilisation transcending the barriers of caste, religion, sex and disparities of wealth and surmounting social disabilities and disadvantages.

P.K. Thungon committee

In the year 1988, planning commission appointed a working group on district planning and the Thungon committee was a sub committee of the working group. It was mainly assigned to recommend ways and means to strengthen the panchayati raj institutions. The committee gave some suggestions to revitalise the panchayati raj institutions.

This committee also proposed the reservation policy for the weaker sections of the society on the basis of population. It also suggested the 37% reservation of the seats of chairman and vice chairman for the scheduled castes and scheduled tribes at each level of panchayati raj institutions. In the case of small size institution, the committee suggested for only one seat for a women member.

64th Constitutional Amendment Bill (1989)

To provide the constitutional support to the panchayati raj institutions, a Constitutional Amendment Bill was introduced in 1989 by Sri Rajiv Gandhi the then P.M., with an intention of transferring power to the people. It relates to part IX of the constitution. This bill was passed by the Lok Sabha on the 10th August 1989. However it failed in Rajya Sabha and could not become the part of the constitution.

The main objectives of the bill as pointed out in the statement by the Rajiv Gandhi were, to remove the inadequacies such as, failure to hold regular and periodic elections, prolonged suppressions, inadequate representation to the weaker sections like the SC and ST and Women, lack of financial resources and inadequate devolution of powers and responsibilities on them. Prime Minister Rajiv Gandhi claimed that this bill was a historic and revolutionary bill and its introduction in Lok Sabha was the single greatest even after the enactment of the constitution.

The main provisions of the proposed constitution Amendment bill were as follows:

1. There will be three tier system of panchayats at village, intermediate and district levels of states.
2. Regular elections after every 5 year would be held under the supervision of the chief election commission. If a panchayati raj body was dismissed for some reason it must be reconstituted through election within 6 months.
3. All seats of panchayati raj bodies would be filled by direct elections. State legislature may appoint MPs, MLAs and other as ex-officio members of Panchayati raj institutions without the voting power.
4. 30% seats would be reserved for women in panchayati raj institutions. And reservation of seats for SC/ST would be in proportion to the population in the total population.
5. Preparation of plans for economic development and social justice of the people by the panchayati raj institutions.
6. To provide the adequate financial resources to panchayati raj institutions by the state government in the form of grants. And panchayati raj institutions also be

empowered to levy some taxes, duties, toll and fees for their resources.

7. State finance commission would be set up to review the finance of the panchayats and it also recommend the principles on the basis of which state legislature may determine the taxes to be appropriated by or assigned to the panchayats.
8. To supervise the accounts and audit of expenditure of panchayats by the Comptroller and Auditor General.

After the defeat of both the bills, another bill that is 73rd constitution amendment Bill was introduced in the Lok Sabha.

73rd Constitutional Amendment Act

The attempt extending the constitutional benefits to the panchayat raj institutions, thoroughly the 64th Constitutional Amendment Act of 1988 and 74th Amendment Bill of 1990 did not succeed. Another attempt was made by introducing the Constitutional Amendment Bill on 16th September 1991. After the series of discussions in the parliament, the matter was referred to joint select committee of parliament for detailed examination. Accordingly joint committee presented its report to parliament in July 1992. The Lok Sabha finally passed the bill on December 22nd, 1992 and the Raja Sabha on December 23rd, 1992. The President of India accorded this asset on April 20th, 1993. Finally the 73rd constitutional amendment act of 1992 came into effect on April 24th, 1993.

Salient features of 73rd Amendment Act

The Constitutional (73rd Amendment) Act provides for establishment of three tiers of Panchayats as units of local self-government. It also contains provisions regarding regular elections to Panchayat bodies, setting up of a State Election Commission and a State Finance Commission, reservation for SCs, STs and women, enabling provisions for the reservation for backward classes and citizens, etc. Sufficient powers and responsibilities were to be developed upon these institutions at appropriate levels to enable them to prepare and implement the schemes for economic development and social justice.

Gram Sabha: The Gram Sabha has been envisaged as the foundation of the Panchayati Raj system. It shall perform such functions and exercise such powers as may be ensured to it by the State legislatures.

There shall be three tiers of Panchayats at the village, intermediate and district levels. So, only those states having population not exceeding 20 lakhs have the discretion not to constitute the panchayats at the intermediate level. Under Article 243 the President can make special dispensation for Union Territories.

Direct elections: All seats in a panchayat at every level are to be filled by direct elections from territorial constituencies demarcated for this purpose, with the ratio between the population of such constituency and the number of such constituency and the number of seats allotted to it being the same throughout the Panchayat area. Reservation of seats: There shall be reservation of seats at every level for SC/STs in proportion to their population in a given Panchayat area and *for* women to the extent of not less than one-third of the total number of seats. Likewise, the office of the Chairpersons in the Panchayats at each level shall be reserved for women, to the extent of not less than one-third of the total numbers in the office of Chairpersons of Panchayats. In addition, the legislature of any state can make provision for reservation of seats in any panchayats at any level in favour of the Backward Class.

Five year term: The term of office of panchayat at every level shall be for five years and if dissolved earlier or on expiry of the term, elections must be completed within six months from the date of dissolution or expiry.

Finance commission: By 24th April 1993, that is, the coming into the effect the constitutional (73rd Amendment) Act, 1992 and thereafter at the expiration of every fifth year, a finance commission shall be constituted in every fifth year. A finance commission shall be constituted in every state to go into the governing principles of the distribution and revolution of financial resources between the state and the panchayats at every level and the measures to improve the financial position of the panchayats.

State election commission: The direction and control of the preparation of electoral rolls and the conduct of all elections in the panchayats shall be vested in a state election commission, to be constituted by the state concerned.

Eleventh Schedule: Finally, the XI Schedule comprising 29 items has been added to the Constitution which ought to provide an effective role to the PRIs in the planning and implementation of works of local significance. Activities ranging like drinking water, agriculture, land and water conservation to communications, poverty alleviation programmes, family welfare, education, libraries and cultural activities, maintenance of community as sets etc.

States and areas kept out of the Act: The Constitutional (73rd Amendment) Act, 1992 does not apply to the States of Meghalaya, Mizoram and Nagaland and certain other areas as specified in the Article 243 M. These areas include Scheduled Areas under Article 244(1), tribal areas under Article 244(2), Hill Areas of Manipur for which District Councils Acts exists and the district of Darjeeling in the State of West Bengal, for which Darjeeling Gorkha Hill Council exists. It is interesting to note that the hill areas of Manipur which comprise the entire State except the three valley districts of Imphal, Thoubal and Bishnupur are neither convered by the V Schedule nor by the VII Schedule to the Constitution.

Governor's power: While pondering over this issue, the powers given to the Governor in the V Schedule to the Constitution provides that the Governor may, by public notification, direct that any particular Act of Parliament or of Legislature of the state. Which shall apply or shall not apply, with such exemptions and modifications as may be specified, to the Scheduled Areas or to any part there of. It is obvious that the new Panchayat Raj legislation passed by the respective States can be straight way extended by the Governor of the State concerned to the Scheduled Areas with such modifications as may be deemed necessary, after consulting the respective Tribal Advisory Councils.

Clause 5(2) of the V Schedule provides that the Governor may make regulation for peace and good government for any area in the State, which, for the time being, is a Scheduled Area. This provision is, therefore, contained in the Constitution to cater the need of peace and good government in these areas and in this regard the Governor alone can decide its necessity. The Governor's power to legislate extends to all the three lists of the VII Schedule to the Constitution.

Restriction: The only restriction on the exercise of the powers conferred under clause 5 of the Schedule is that the regulation must be in prior consultation with the Tribal Advisory Council, if there is any such Council and should be submitted for the President's assent. Without the President's assent a regulation under Clause 5(2) would not have any effect.

Universal application: Article 245 (1) of the Constitution provides that an Act of Parliament or the State Legislature applies of its own force, to the whole of the territory of India or the State, as the case may be.

The alternative

While this is the substantive position obtaining from the V Schedule, the provisions contained in Article 243 M (4) (b) empowers Parliament to extend by law, the provisions of Part IX of the Constitution to the Scheduled Areas and the tribal areas referred under Article 234 M (1), subject to such exception and modification as may be specified in such law. No such law shall be deemed to be an Amendment of the Constitution for the purpose of Article 368.

Legislation proposed: In June, 1994, the Government of the India's Ministry of Rural Development, constituted a Committee of select MP's and Experts to make recommendations on the salient features of the law for extending the provisions of Part IX of the Constitution to the Scheduled Areas. This Committee submitted its report on January 1995. It favours legislation by Parliament under Article 243 M (4) (b) of the Constitution.

The intention of the constitution appears to extend to these areas suitable measures to be evolved after considering the special circumstances prevailing there. This could be achieved by the special provision to be introduced by the Governor under Clause 5 for the V Schedule to the Constitution or through a Central law to be passed by Parliament under Article 243 M (4) (b). This purpose of the Constitution does not appear to have been adequately appreciated by the States because Governors have rarely exercised the powers under Clause 5 of the V Schedule. This prompts the perception that Parliament should legislate under Article 243 M (4) (b) although it sounds paradoxical that a Central law for decentralisation is favoured.[14]

In short, it can be said that the act provides for establishment of three types of Panchayats as units of local self government. It also contains provisions regarding regular elections to Panchayat bodies, setting up of a State Election Commission and State Finance Commission, reservation for SCs/STs and women, provision for reservations for backward classes of citizen's etc. According to the latest position.

Panchayat Raj institution system has been statutorily provided fully or partially in 22 out of 25 States and in 6 out of 7 Union territories. In remaining three States and one Union territory there are traditional tribal councils. And of the 22 states, only 15 states have three-tier system. These states are Andhra Pradesh, Arunachal Pradesh, Assam, Bihar, Gujarat, Himachal Pradesh, Karnataka, Madhya Pradesh, Maharashtra, Orissa, Punjab, Rajasthan, Tamil Nadu, Uttar Pradesh and West Bengal. The two-tier system has been statutorily provided in the states of Kerala, Haryana, Manipur and Sikkim. In Goa, Jammu and Kashmir and Tripura there is only one-tier system. There are 217,300 village panchayats, existing in 22 Sates and three union territories, covering about 96% of 5,79,000 villages. It covers nearly 99.6% rural population.

There has been an increasing trend in some states to re-empower the PRI, to undertake special development programmes along with the usual civic and welfare functions. Many states are yet to provide state finance commission.

The actual status and functioning of PR continues to be uneven across the states. Maharashtra, Gujarat, West Bengal, Karnataka and Andhra Pradesh have had a good record of effective functioning of PRI. Other states are yet to gear up their machinery for the success of PRI.

The Union Government had taken steps towards the implementation of 73rd Amendment Act. It convened a Conference of State Ministers and Administrative Secretaries in charge of PR to evolve an action plan. The Communication of Prime Minister regarding the significance of the PR Act, has been communicated to all the chairman of PRIs.

References

1. Quoted in Sakuntala Sharma, *Grass Root Politics and Panchayati Raj*, Deep and Deep Publications, 1994, p. 88.
2. Quoted in Vasant Desai, *Panchayati Raj, Power to the People*, Himalaya Publishing House, Bombay, Delhi, 1990, p. 50.

3. Quoted in B.L. Tak, *Sociological Dimensions of Gram Raj*, Vimal Prakashan, Ghaziabad, 1973, p. 3.
4. Bhatnagar, S, *Rural Local Government in India*, Light of Life Publications, New Delhi, 1978, p. 18.
5. Quoted in High Tinker, *The Foundations of Local Self-Government in India, Pakistan and Burma*, Kalvani Publishing House, Bombay, 1967.
6. Majumdar, R.C. and Others, *An advanced History of India*, Macmillian and Co., London, 1970, p. 556.
7. Quoted in R.L. Khanna, *Panchayati raj in India*, the English book depot, Ambala Cantt, 1970, p. 26.
8. Ram Reddy, G, "Panchayat Raj and Rural Development in Andhra Pradesh, India" in Norman T. Uphoff, *Rural Development and Local Organisation in Asia*, Macmillan India Ltd., Delhi, 1982, p. 78.
9. Maheshwari, S.R., *Local Government in India*, Laskhminarayana Aggrawal, Agra, 1988, p. 61.
10. Report of the Team for this study of community project and National Extension Service, Vol. I., New Delhi, Committee on Plan Project, 1957, p. 7.
11. Barthwal, C.P., *Public Administration in India*, Ashish Publishing House, New Delhi, 1993, p. 306.
12. Vasant Desai, *Panchayati Raj Power to the People*, Himalaya Publishing House, Bombay, 1990, p. 386. 13.
13. The Karnataka Zilla Parishads and Taluka Panchayats Samitis, Mandal panchayats and Nayay Panchayats Act, 1985 Dept. of Law and Parliamentary Affairs, Government of Karnataka, Bangalore.
14. *Ibid.*
15. Sweeta Mishra, *Democratic Decentralisation in India*, Mittal Publications, New Delhi, 1994, p. 67.
16. Duby, A.K., Panchayati Raj, The Constitutional perspective in Kurukshetra, April 1995, p. 108-112.

Chapter - III

Panchayati Raj System in Andhra Pradesh

One of the tasks of nation building and development, writes Milton J. Esman is to bring members of the national community into a network of relationships and institutions which enable them to participate actively in decisions affecting their individual and group welfare while this is true of all nations, it has posed a considerable problem to the developing nations like India. The principle that members of the national community should have an opportunity to participate actively in decisions affecting their lives is accepted by most of the persons charged with the responsibility of shaping the policies.[1] In this context Panchayati Raj as a system of rural local administration has come a long way since its inception in the late 1950s as a corrective to the lapse noted in the working of the bureaucratically dominated community development programme initiated in the early 1950s as a corrective to the lapse noted in the working of the bureaucratically dominated community development programme initiated in the early 1950s[2]. An organically linked-up three –tier system of village panchayats. Panchayat samithis and zilla parishads was installed in quick succession in several states[3] as a sequel to the recommendation of Balwant Ray Mehta study team report of 1957. With the introduction of the panchayati Raj institutions there was a shift from bureaucratic administration to democratic administration. The idea of adopting this system was to have a democratic approach and to place the administration in the hands of both the officials and elected representatives so as to make them partners in the development process. This was a new experiment in the sphere of rural local government administration. The system formulates and executes development programmes through people's participation and instills political consciousness among the rural people[4]. These panchayati Raj institutions emerged as the institutions of socio-economic, political and cultural development with the provision of effective people's participation in policy formulation and implementation at the grassroots level.

Andhra Pradesh is one of the first two states [5] in the country to establish the panchayati Raj set-up in 1959 much on the lines of the Balwant Ray Mehta Committee Report. The experience of Panchayati Raj in Andhra Pradesh is nearly three and a half decades old during this period[6], the Government of Andhra Pradesh appointed several commissions and committees and made attempts to improve the functioning of the Panchayati Raj have become moribund (and) they have been denuded of their promise and vitality.[7] The committee felt that the institutions of Panchayati Raj 'have to be viewed as institutions of self-government which would naturally facilitate the participation of the people in the process of planning and development flowing from and as a part of the concept of self government[8]. This committee reiterated the conceptualisation of Panchayats embodied in Article 40 of the constitution [9]. The committee recommended that "local self government should be constitutionally recognised, protected, preserved by the inclusion of a new chapter in the constitution[10]".

In conformity with the Constitution 73rd Amendment Act, 1992 the Andhra Pradesh Legislature enacted the Andhra Pradesh Panchayati Raj Act-1994. It repealed three of its earlier Acts relating to the Panchayats Act, 1964, Andhra Pradesh Mandal praja parishads, Zilla Praja parishads and Zilla pranalika and Abhivrudhi Mandals Act 1986 and Andhra Pradesh Local Bodies Electoral Reforms Act, 1989.

Thus, the new Act reintroduced a three tier system of Panchayati Raj constituting zill parishads (ZPs) at the district level, Mandal parishads (MPs) at the intermediary level and Gram Panchayat (GPs) at the village level by merging the Andhra Pradesh Gram Panchayats Act, 1964 and Andhra Pradesh Abhivrudhi and Sameseeksha Mandals Act 1986.

The present pattern of Panchayati Raj in the state is functioning under the Andhra Pradesh Panchayati Raj Act 1994. Keeping in view the past experiences it became imperative to provide constitutional status to local self-government to impart certainty, continuity and strength. The Constitution's 73rd Amendment essentially lays down certain ground values with basic structural framework so that it can sustain against external interference and could establish themselves as effective and strong people's institutions.

The powers and functions of the Panchayati Raj institutions are on the lines of the 73rd Amendment Act. All the 29 items included in the Eleventh Schedule inserted by the 73rd constitutional Amendment Act find a place in Schedule I of the Andhra Pradesh Panchayati Raj Act, 1994. The subjects mentioned in Schedule I of the Act are common to all the three tiers of the Panchayati Raj Institutions.

Structure of the Panchayati Raj System:

Gram panchayat:

Constitution of a Gram panchayat:

The Gram panchayat is the body constituted for a village[11] the administration of a village is vested in Gram Panchayat[12] Every Gram Panchayat is a body corporate by the name of the village with a perpetual succession and a common seal. As a corporate body[13] it can sue and can be sued in a court of law.

It can acquire and hold and transfer its property and can enter into contracts to discharge its duties under the Act. The term of office of the Gram Panchayat is five years.

Strength of a Gram Panchayat

According to a provision of the Act[14] - A Gram Panchayat shall consist of such number of elected members inclusive of its Sarpanch as may be notified from time to time, by the commissioner. The number of members notified in the table.

Gram Panchayat with a population at the time of last Census	Number of members
(1)	(2)
Up to 300	5
Exceeding 300 but not exceeding 500	7
Exceeding 500 but not exceeding 1,500	9
Exceeding 1,500 but not exceeding 3,000	11
Exceeding 3,000 but not exceeding 5,000	13
Exceeding 5000 but not exceeding 10,000	15
Exceeding 10,000 but not exceeding 15,000	17
Exceeding 15,000	Between 19 and 21

Source: AP Panchayati Raj Act, 1994, p. 15.

Election of Members

All members of the Gram Panchayat are elected by the registered voters in the ward by the method of secret ballot[15]. The act has adopted two children norm as a qualification for the members of the panchayat. In addition, all other members except women who are absent for a period of ninety days from the date of the commencement of the term of office or absent for three ordinary meetings continuously are disqualified. In the case of women a period of not less than four months at a time is excluded if the lady is physically disabled or due to advanced stage of pregnancy and delivery.

Reservation of seats of members of Gram Panchayat

In every Gram Panchayat out of the total strength of elected members the seats are reserved[16] to Scheduled Castes and Scheduled Tribes subject to the condition that the number of seats so reserved shall bear the same proportion to the total number of seats to be filled by the direct election to the Gram Panchayat. Such reserved seats for scheduled castes and scheduled tribes are allotted by rotation to different wards in a Gram Panchayat, besides, allotted by rotation to different wards in a Gram Panchayat. Besides, One-third of seats are reserved for women[17] who include those belonging to scheduled castes and scheduled tribes based on their population ratio. The amendment No. 5, dated February 3rd, 1995 to the Act. Stipulated reservation of not less than thirty-four percent of the seats for the backward classes.[18]

The Sarpanch

Election and Term

The Sarpanch of the Gram Panchayat is directly elected by the people enrolled in electoral rolls for the Gram Panchayat[19] through the method of secret ballot on non-party basis. The election of the Sarpanch may be held at the same time and in the same place as the ordinary elections of the members of the Gram Panchayat.[20] As per the Act, the term of office of the Sarpanch who is elected at an ordinary election shall be five years from the date appointed by the election authority for the first meeting of the Gram Panchayat after the ordinary election.[21] Any casual vacancy in the office of the Sarpanch shall be filled within 120 days from the date of occurrence of such vacancy by a fresh election. And a person elected as Sarpanch in any such vacancy shall hold office only so long as the person in whose place he is elected would have been entitled to hold office if the vacancy had not occurred.[22]

It is to be noted that no casual vacancy in the office of the Sarpanch shall be filled within six months before the date on which the ordinary election of the sarpanch shall be held[23] unless the competent authority (Commissioner appointed for that purpose under the Act) so directs. The Act clearly lays down that a person is not qualified[24] to contest for the office of the Sarpanch, if he is less than 21 years of age; and if his name is not included in the electoral rolls of the village to which he contests. A person shall be disqualified for election as Sarpanch if he is in arrears of any dues, or is interested in a contract within the jurisdiction of the Mandal Parishad in which his village lies.

Reservation

The office of the Sarpanch is again reserved[25] for different categories of people like Scheduled Castes, Scheduled Tribes, Women and Backward Classes on the scale of reservation adopted for electing the members.

Upa- Sarpanch

One of the persons is elected as the Upa-Sarpanch from amongst the members. When the office of the Sarpanch is vacant, the Upa-Sarpanch exercises the powers and performs the function of the Sarpanch until a new Sarpanch is elected and assumes office.

Powers and Functions of the Sarpanch

The Sarpanch has powers and functions[26] specified by the Act, besides, the Sarpanch has the emergency powers.[27]

The Sarpanch

(a) Is responsible for making arrangements to the election of the Upa-Sarpanch.

(b) Has access to the records of the gram panchayat.

(c) Exercise administrative control over the executive officer for the purpose of implementation of the resolutions of the Gram Panchayat or its committee.

(d) Has power to get information from any village secretary of any village within the jurisdiction of the Gram Panchayat.

(e) Is responsible for intimating to the District Panchayat Officer as to the disqualifications of the members of the panchayat.

(f) Acts within the resolution of the Gram Panchayat.

(g) Can devolve the powers and functions to Upa- Sarpanch as per the Act.

(h) Can direct any executive work of the gram panchayat in the interest of general public. However, he is required to inform the same to the gram committee in the ensuing meeting. This refers to the emergency powers of the Sarpanch.

Classification of Gram Panchayats

Coming to Gram Panchayats in the state, they are, interestingly, classified into (a) notified Gram Panchayats, and (b) non-notified Gram Panchayats on the basis of their annual income. The notified Gram Panchayats are again classified into (a) group-1 notified Gram Panchayat (with an annual income of over Rs 60,000 and (b) group-II notified Gram Panchayats (with an annual income of more than Rs 40,000 but less than Rs 60,000). The notified Gram Panchayats have an executive officer and assisted by clerks-cum-bill collectors, sanitary inspector, etc. The staffing pattern of the non-notified Gram Panchayats comprised part-time bill collectors and part-time sweepers only.

Functions of Gram Panchayat

Apart from the functions mentioned in the eleventh Schedule of the constitution (73rd Amendment) Act, the Panchayat Act listed out a wide array of functions of the Gram Panchayat. They included 12 obligatory functions and

27 optional functions. The obligatory functions include the civil functions of construction, lighting of roads and sanitary services, records relating to births and deaths, prevention and remedy of epidemics etc. While development and welfare measures such as maintenance of dispensaries, primary schools, libraries, parks, family relief, public markets etc., are included in the discretionary list of functions.

The duty of gram panchayat is to carry out the requirements of the village. Fro example, construction, repair and maintenance of all buildings of the gram panchayat and the panchayat public roads of the village, bridges, culverts, road, dams and causeways, the lighting of public roads and public places, the construction of drains and their maintenance, the cleaning of streets, and water resources, public latrines, maintenance of burial grounds and the disposal of unclaimed dead bodies etc.

Functional committees

The Act provides for the setting up of functional up of fictional committees including of joint committees of Gram Panchayat on various subjects like agriculture, public health, water supply, sanitation, family planning, education and communication. Interestingly, there is also a provision for a Beneficiary committee for the Gram Panchayat. The Act says that for every gram panchayat there shall be a committee by name Beneficiary committee for the execution of the works of the Gram Panchayat.

Gram Sabha (GS)

A Gram Sabha is constituted for every village and consists of all persons whose names are included in the electoral role of the Gram Panchayat. The Gram Sabha meets at least twice in a year for considering the following matters.

(a) Annual statement of accounts and audit reports.

(b) Report on the administration of the proceeding year.

(c) Programme of works for the year or any new programmes not covered by the budget as the annual programme.

(d) Proposals for fresh taxation or for enhancement of existing taxes.

(e) Selection of schemes, beneficiaries and locations, and

(f) Such other matters as may be prescribed.

The Gram Panchayat shall give due consideration to the suggestions made by the gram sabha.

All the meetings of the Gram Sabha are covered by the Executive officer and will be presided over by the Sarpanch, or in the absence of the Sarpanch, by the upa-sarpanch of the Gram Panchayat it is to be noted that the sabha has an advisory role to play in respect of accounts and audit reports, annual administrative report on the working of the panchayat, imposition of new taxes, selection of beneficiaries under different programmes etc.

Mandal Parishads

Constitution and composition of a Mandal Parishad

The Mandal Parishad (MP) is constituted for each Mandal. Every Mandal Parishad is a body corporate having perpetual succession and a common seal with power to acquire, hold and dispose of property and to enter into contracts and may by its corporate names and be sued.

A Mandal Parishad, *inter alia* consists of:

(a) Members elected from territorial constituencies,

(b) Members of Legislative Assembly representing a constituency which comprises either whole or part of the Mandal concerned –ex-officio,

(c) Members of the House of the People representing a constituency which comprises whole or part of the Mandal concerned –ex-officio,

(d) Member of the Council of States who is a registered voter in a Mandal-ex-officio,
(e) One member belonging to minorities and co-opted by the elected members, and
(f) Sarpanch of Gram Panchayats as permanent invitees.

Members of Mandal Parishad

Elected from territorial constituencies

Each Mandal Parishad is divided into Mandal Parishad Territorial constituencies. For the purpose of election of members from territorial constituencies, each constituency consists of population between 3,000-4,000. One member shall be elected to the Mandal Parishad from each territorial constituency by the persons who are registered voters in the territorial constituency concerned. Any registered voter in the Mandal Parishad is eligible to contest from any territorial constituency of the Mandal Parishad[36]. A person is eligible for election as member of a Mandal Parishad if completes the age of 21 years and must be enrolled as an elector in the offices of president /vice-president of Mandal Parishad. A member elected at an ordinary election or a co-opted member shall hold office for a term of five years from the date of appointment.

Reservation

In every Mandal Parishad, out of the total strength of elected members the seats are reserved to scheduled castes and scheduled tribes subject to the condition that the number of seats so reserved shall bear the same proportion to the total number of seats to be filled by the direct election to the Mandal Parishad. Such reserved seats for scheduled castes and scheduled tribes are allotted by rotation to different constituencies in a Mandal Parishad. Besides one-third of seats are reserved for women who include those belonging to scheduled castes and scheduled tribes based on their population ratio.

Mandal President

The president and vice-president of each Mandal Parishad are elected by the elected members of the Mandal Parishad. The term of office of the president or vice-president who is elected at an ordinary election is five years. The term of office of the president or vice-president has to be filled within a period of six months by fresh election.

Powers and functions

The Mandal Parishad president has the power to:

(a) exercise the administrative control over the Mandal Parishad Development Officer for implementing the resolution of the Mandal Parishad;

(b) preside over and conduct meeting of the Mandal Parishad;

(c) access all the records of the Mandal Parishad;

(d) direct the execution of any work in the interest of the general public subject to the provisions of the Act. This is the emergency power of the president of a Mandal Parishad.

The vice-president of a Mandal Parishad exercises powers and performs functions of the president, as the president may from time to time delegate to him in writing when the office of the president is vacant, the vice-president of a Mandal Parishad exercise the powers and functions of the president until a new president is elected.

The collector and the president of agricultural marketing committees are the permanent invitees to the meetings of the Mandal Parishad with right to speak but are not entitled to vote in any meeting the Mandal Parishad Development Officer (MPDO) is the overall in charge of administration. He is supported by the following personnel at the Mandal Parishad level— Mandal Engineering Officer, Mandal Education Officer,

Extension Officer (Rural Development), Village Development Officer (men), Village Development Officer (Women), Senior Assistant, Junior Assistants, works inspector, Typist etc.

Power and Functions of Mandal Parishad

Every Mandal Parishad can exercise many powers and perform such functions as may be entrusted to it by rules made in this behalf in regard to the subjects enumerated in Schedule I and particularly exercise powers and perform functions specified in Schedule II. There are 29 items under Schedule I whereas the function under schedule II are classified under broad categories of (1) community development, (2) Agriculture (3) Animal Husbandry and Fisheries, and (4) Health and Rural sanitation. Under community development the execution of all programmes in association with panchayats, cooperative societies, voluntary organisations and the people.

Under agriculture, the doing of everything necessary to step up agricultural production and in particular multiplication and distribution of improved seeds, distribution of fertilisers, popularisation of improved techniques etc.

Under Animal husbandry and Fisheries, comes upgrading local stock by introducing pedigree breeding bulls and castrating scrub bulls, improved breeds of cattle sheep, pigs and poultry, controlling contagious diseases, establishing and maintaining veterinary dispensaries etc.

Under health and rural sanitation were included, expanding existing medical and health service and bring them within the reach of the people, establishing and maintaining primary health centers and maternity centres; providing protected drinking water facilities; ensuring systematic vaccination controlling epidemics; providing drains etc in this way, a wide range of subjects have been entrusted to the Mandal Parishad without demarcating the sphere of action of each item. The Mandal Parishad, if needed, with prior approval of the Zilla Parishad can levy contributions from funds of the Gram Panchayats I and the Mandal. Broadly speaking, the functions of the Mandal Parishad consists of functions related to development, social welfare and social security. As per section 175 of the Act, each Mandal Parishad can appoint one or more joint committees for any activity.

Mandal Parishad Fund

Every Mandal Parishad is equipped with Mandal Parishad fund and all money received by a Mandal Parishad constitute a fund called the Mandal Parishad fund. All moneys received by the Mandal Parishad are lodged into the nearest government treasury. The Mandal Parishad development officer is empowered to sign all orders or cheques to withdraw moneys from and out of the Mandal Parishad fund.

The sources of income to the Mandal Parishad consist of:

1. The Government or heads of the Department of the government to the Mandal Parishad.
2. Funds relating to the community development programmes, central and state aid received from the all India Bodies and Organisations for the development of cottage and village industries, khadi, silk, coir, handy crafts and the like.
3. Donations and contributions received by the Mandal Parishad from Gram Panchayats or from the public in any form.
4. Such income of Zilla Parishad as the Government may by order allocate to it.
5. Such share of the land revenue state taxes or fees as may be prescribed.
6. Proceeds from taxes, surcharges. Or fee which the Mandal Parishad is empowered to levy under this act; and

7. Any other income from Remunerative Enterprises and the like.

Mandal Development Officer

The Mandal Parishad Development Officer is the chief executive officer of the Mandal Parishad. He is responsible for implementing the resolutions of the Mandal Parishad. He exercises powers of supervision over the gram panchayats. The Mandal Parishad development officer convenes the meeting of the Mandal Parishad with the approval of the Mandal Parishad president. He takes part in the meetings of the Mandal Parishad and is not entitled to vote or move any resolution. He exercises administrative control over the staff of the Mandal Parishad office. The political head of the Mandal Parishad is the president while the Mandal Development Officer is the administrative head.

Zilla Parishad

Constitution of a Zilla Parishad

A Zilla Parishad is constituted by the government by notification for a district. Every Zilla Parishad is constituted by the name of the district for which it is constituted. It is a body corporate having perpetual succession and a common seal with power to acquire, hold and dispose of property and to enter into contracts. It can sue and can be sued in a court of law.

A Zilla Parishad consists of:

(a) Members elected from territorial constituencies which obviously are a Mandal.

(b) Member of Legislative Assembly of the state representing a constituency which forms a part or a whole of the district concerned.

(c) Member of the House of the People representing a constituency which forms a part or a whole of the district concerned.

(d) Member of the Legislative Council of the state who is registered voter in the district, and

(e) Two members belonging to minorities and co-opted by the elected members of the Zilla Parishad.

The chairman, district cooperative marketing society, chairman, Zilla Granthalaya samstha; chairman, District cooperative central Bank; District collector; and all presidents of Mandal Parishad in the district, are the permanent invitees to the meetings of the Zilla Parishad. These members are entitled to participate in the meetings of the Zilla Parishad without the right to vote.

Power and functions of Zilla Parishad

According to the provision of the Act 1994, the Zilla Parishad is enjoined upon to perform the functions out of the 29 items entrusted to it by the rules, the Zilla Parishad is also responsible for securing coordination between all the rural local bodies in the district besides advising the government on rural development works in the district besides advising the government on rural development works in the district, and distribution of funds between the 3-tiers of PR.

The Zilla Parishad has power to:

(a) Examine and approve the budget of Mandal Parishad in the district.

(b) Distribute the funds allotted to the district by the central and the state to the Mandal Parishad.

(c) Coordinate and consolidate the plans prepared in respect of the Mandals in the district, and prepare plans in respect of the entire district.

(d) Secure the execution of the plans, projects, schemes and other works either solely relating to the individuals, Mandals or common to two or more Mandals in the district.

(e) Supervise generally the activities of the Mandal Parishad in the district.

(f) Exercise and perform the powers and functions of the district board including the powers to levy any tax or fees as may be transferred to it by the state Government.

(g) Exercise and perform other powers and functions in relation to any development programme as the Government may by notification confer on it or entrust to it.

(h) Advise government on all matters relating to development activities and maintenance of services in the district whether undertaken by local authorities or government.

(i) Advise government on the allocation of work among grama panchayats and Mandal Parishad and coordination of work between the said bodies and among the various gram panchayats themselves.

(j) Advise government on matters concerning the implementation of any statutory on executive order specially referred to it by the government.

(k) Collect data and publish statistics relating to local activities.

(l) Require any local authority to furnish information regarding its activities.

(m) Accept trusts relating to exclusively the furtherance of any purpose for which its funds may be applied.

(n) Establish, maintain or expand secondary, vocational and industrial schools.

Broadly speaking, the function of Zilla Parishad can be classified into executive, supervisory, advisory and co-ordinate functions. The Zilla Parishad functions through various standing Committees.

Standing Committees

For every Zilla Parishad the following Standing Committees are constituted:

(a) Standing committees for planning and finance. The function of the committees is to evolve district plan, budget, taxation, finance proposal and coordination of the work relating to other committees.

(b) Standing Committees for Rural Development. The committee looks after the poverty alleviation programme, area development programmes, employment, housing, cooperation, thrift and small savings, industries including cottage, village and small scale industries and trusts.

(c) Standing Committee for Agriculture. The committee looks after agriculture, animal husbandry. Soil reclamation including contour bonding, social forestry, fisheries and sericulture.

(d) Standing committee for education and medical services. The committee deals with education including social education, medical services, public health and sanitation, including drainage, relief for distress in grave emergencies.

(e) Standing Committee for Woman Welfare. The committee looks after development of women and welfare of children.

(f) Standing Committee for Social Welfare. The committee looks after social welfare for scheduled castes, scheduled tribes and backward classes and cultural affairs.

(g) Standing Committee for Works. This committee looks after communications, rural water supply, power and irrigation.

Thus, here are seven standing committees for planning and finance, rural development, agriculture, education and medical services, women's welfare, social welfare activities and works of the Zilla Parishad.

Chairman and Vice-chairman of the Zilla Parishad

The Chairman and Vice chairman of the Zilla Parishad are elected by the elected members of the Zilla Parishad.

There is a provision of reservation to the office of the chairman of the Zilla Parishad. Out of the total number of offices of chairperson to the Zilla Parishads in the state the number of offices are reserved by to ratio to the members belonging to the Scheduled Castes and Scheduled Tribes in proportion to their population in the state, the reservation of offices in favour of Scheduled Castes, Scheduled Tribes, Backward Classes and women and the unreserved offices in the three areas of the state viz., Coastal Andhra, Telengana and Rayalaseema:

Name of the Area	Scheduled Castes	Scheduled Tribes	Backward Classes	Unreserved Seats	Total
Costal Andhra					
(a) Men or Women	1	1	2	2	6
(b) Women	1	-	1	1	3
Telengana					
(a) Men or Women	1	-	2	3	6
(b) Women	-	1	1	1	3
Rayalaseema					
(a) Men or Women	-	-	1	1	2
(b) Women	1	-	-	1	2
Total	4	2	7	9	22

Source: AP Panchayati Raj Act, 1994, pp. 139-140.

The above table shows that number of offices reserved for scheduled castes is approximately eighteen percent of the total number of offices of chairman in the state. The number of offices reserved for Scheduled Tribes is approximately eight percent of the total number of offices of chairman in state. The number of seats reserved for backward classes is approximately one-third of the total number of offices of chairman in the state. The number of offices reserved for women is approximantely one-third of the total number of offices reserved for Scheduled Castes, Scheduled Tribes, Backward Classes and the Unreserved seats. The reservation of offices of the Chairman to all the categories put together is in the ratio of 2:2:1 in respect of the three regions of the state viz., Coastal Andhra, Telengana and Rayalaseema respectively.

Powers and Functions of Zilla Parishad Chairman and Vice-Chairman

The chairman of Zilla Parishad exercises administrative controls over the chief executive officer for the purpose of implementation of the resolutions of the Zilla Parishad or any of its Standing committees. The chairman has the power to preside over and conduct the meeting of the Zilla Parishad, the chairperson has full access of all records of the Zilla Parishad.

The Vice-Chairman exercises such power and performs such functions of the Chairman as the chairman may from time of time delegate to him in writing. When the office of the Chairman is vacant the Vice-chairman of the Zilla Parishad shall exercise the powers and performs the functions, if the Chairman until a new chairman is elected, if the chairman has been continuously absent from the district for more than fifteen days or is incapacitated for more than fifteen days. His powers and functions during such absence or incapacity shall devolve in the vice-chairman.

Funds of the Zilla Parishad

Every Zilla Parishad is equipped with a Zilla Parishad Fund. All money received by a Zilla Parishad constitute a fund called the Zilla Parishad Fund, all moneys received by the Zilla Parishad are lodged into the nearest Government Treasury. The Chief Executive Officer is empowered to sign all orders of cheques to withdraw moneys from and out of the Mandal Parishad fund.

The sources of income to the Parishad Fund:

(1) The Central or State Government Funds allotted to the Zilla Parishad.

(2) Grants from All India bodies and institutions for the development of cottage, and small scale industries and the like.

(3) Prescribed Share of the State Taxes or Fees.

(4) Proceeds from taxes of fees levied and collected by the Zilla Parishad under law.

(5) Income from endowments of trusts administered by the Zilla Parishad.

(6) Donations and contributions from the Mandal Parishad or from the Public in any form.

(7) Any other income from Remunerative Enterprises and the like.

(8) Income through Grants-in-aid.

Chief Executive Officer

There is a Chief Executive Officer in each Zilla Parishad. He is appointed by the state Government to oversee the administration of the Zilla Parishad. He is the administrative head if the Zilla Parishad who works under the control of the Zilla Parishad Chairman who is the Political head. The chief executive officer attends the meeting of the Zilla Parishad and its Standing committees. He takes part in the discussions of the council and its committees but he has no right to vote. He can call for any officer or servant of or holding office under the Zilla Parishad or a Mandal Parishad.

The chief executive officer has power to exercise supervision and control over the acts of the officers and servants holding office under the Zilla Parishad and its institutions in matters of administration. He is the custodian of all records of the Zilla Parishad and its Standing committees. He is responsible for the implementation of the resolutions of the Zilla Parishad and its Standing committees. He is the competent authority to enter into agreements and to sign and execute them in the name and on behalf of the Zilla Parishad from time to time. This is made necessary for the continuity of administration.

The chief executive officer convenes the meetings of the Zilla Parishad with the approval of the Zilla Parishad Chairman. He is supported by the following personnel, viz., (1) Deputy CEO, (2) Accounts Officer, (3) Parishad Education Officer and (4) Executive Engineers. The subordinate staff at the Z.P. level includes Divisional Accounts Officer, Superintendents, Senior Assistants, Junior Assistants, Typist Record Assistants etc.

The analysis of the system of the Panchayat Raj institutions in Andhra Pradesh vide the new A.P. Panchayati Raj Act. 1994 indicates that it incorporates all the mandatory provisions of the 73rd Constitution Amendment Act. Place of Farm Sabha, 3-tier institutions, uniform term of 5 years reservation for SCs and STs in proportion to their one-third reservations for women, similar reservation for chairpersons by rotation, provision for election commission, provision for state finance commission, reconstitution of PRIs with six months in cases of their Dissolution and other related mandatory provisions find place. Institution building at the grass-roots is a democratic exercise 73rd Constitutional Amendment, Act. 1992 has opened a new chapter of meaningfully promises and ideals, assurance and insurance of the existence and continuity of Panchayati Raj and hopefully its stability and sustainability.

References

1. R.V. Jathar, *Evaluation of panchayat raj in India*, Bhatkal Books International, Bombay, 1964. p. 1.
2. S.V. Sampath, Village Panchayats with Special reference to Bombay state, All India Institute of Local Self- government, Bombay, 1957. p. 148.
3. Henry Maddick, *Panchayat Raj: A Study of Rural Local Government*, Longman Group, London, 1970. pp. 71-72, 352-355.
4. Balwant Ray Mehta Committee Report, 1957.

5. Andhra Pradesh Panchayati Samiti and Zilla Parishad Act, 1959. p. 125.
6. Andhra Pradesh Panchayati Samiti and Zilla Parishad Act, 1964. p. 178.
7. The Andhra Pradesh Mandal Praja Parishads, Zilla Praja Parishads, Zilla Pranalika Abhivrudhi Mandals Act 1986, Government of Andhra Pradesh (Act No. 3 of 1986).
8. Anand, C. Prem (Ed), *Panchayat raj in Andhra Pradesh*, Anand Book House, Hyderabad, 1960. p. 193.
9. Report of the State Committee on Panchayat Raj Institutions, Government of Andhra Pradesh, Hyderabad, 1981, p. 241.
10. Ashok Mehata Committee Report, Government of India Report, 1958, p. 241.
11. National Institute of Rural Development, Panchayati Raj Institutions in Selected States: An Analytical Study, NIRD, Hyderabad, 1995. p. 147.
12. *Ibid*, p. 158.
13. M. Devendra Babu, "Status and Working of Panchayats in Andhra Pradesh: Some Preliminary Observations" (Mimeographed), ISEC, Bangalore, August, 1977. p. 48.
14. K.R. Shastri, C.P Vittal and G Ramachandraiah, Panchayati Raj in Andhra Pradesh: An Analytical Study, N I R D, Hyderabad, 1999. p. 7.
15. *Ibid*, p. 29.
16. Haragopal and Sudarshan, Status of Panchayati Raj in the States of India, 1994 (Ed), *Institute of Social Sciences*, Concept Publishing House, New Delhi, 1995. p. 18.
17. Andhra Pradesh Panchayat Raj Act, Government of Andhra Pradesh, Hyderabad, 1994. p. 78.
18. *Ibid.*, p. 82.
19. National Institute of Rural Development, *op. cit.*, p. 139.
20. *Ibid.*, p. 145.
21. Shakuntala Sharma, *Grassroots Politics and Panchayat Raj*, Deep and Deep Publications, New Delhi, 1997. p. 87.
22. *Ibid.*, p. 89.
23. *Ibid.*, p. 91.
24. Andhra Pradesh Panchayat Raj Act, *op. cit.*, p. 76.
25. *Ibid.*, p. 89.

26. E.A. Narayan, *Panchayat Raj in Action: A Study in Context of Andhra Pradesh*, Kapaz Publications, New Delhi, 2008. p. 78.
27. Constitution of Gram Panchayats for Village and their incorporation, Andhra Pradesh Panchayat Raj Act, *op. cit.*, p. 121.

Chapter - IV

Profile of Andhra Pradesh

The successful implementation of any development programmed emphasizes the need for considering the resource base of a particular area. There is also direct correlation between the resource base and enlistment of the communities through various programmes since the available resources in the region have greater effect on the real development process of the area therefore process if the area therefore it is more appropriate to project the study area for understanding its development potentials. The present chapter is accordingly focused on the study area and related aspects. The chapter briefly deals with the salient features of Andhra Pradesh and the study areas such as Anantapur district in Rayalaseema, Warangal in Telangana and West Godawari in Andhra Regions.

(a) The State

Location

On 1st November 1956, the States Reorganisation Act merged the Telugu-speaking areas of the former Hyderabad state also known as Telangana with the Andhra state to form the state of Andhra Pradesh. The city of Hyderabad, the former capital of the Hyderabad State, was made the capital of the new state.

The state of Andhra Pradesh is located between 13° to 20° North latitude and 77° to 85° East longitudes. The state is bound by the Bay of Bengal on the East with a coastline of

974 kilometers, on its northeast by Orissa, in its North by Madhya Pradesh and Maharashtra in its West and Southwest by Karnataka and in its South by Tamil Nadu. Andhra Pradesh is the fifth largest state in the Indian union both in terms of area of as well as population.[1]

The state has area of 2.72 lakhs sq. km forming 804 percent if total geographical area of the country. The state has the longest coastline (974 kms.) among all the littoral states in India.[2]

Map of Andhra Pradesh

Climate

The state has tropical to sub-tropical climate. Humid to semi-humid conditions prevail in the coastal area in the interiors of the state the climate is arid to semi-arid the interior plateau areas have hot summers with relatively pleasant winters.[3] The state receives rainfall mainly from the Southwest monsoon (about 67 percent) and partly from the Northeast monsoon.

Rainfall

The average annual rainfall ranges from 650 mm in semi-arid belt to about 1300 mm in the North Western portion of the state. Rayalaseema region is a zone of low rainfall, recording an average rainfall of 1100 mm and the area north of the Godavari River receives 100-1300 mm of rainfall increases from Southwest of Northeast and also from West to East.[4]

Temperature

The minimum and maximum temperatures of the state generally vary from 13.4°C to 19.7°C and 33.9°C to 42.8°C[5] respectively regional variations in temperature are quite noticeable.

Soils

The state is endowed with a variety if soils ranging from highly fertile and productive deltaic alluvial to black and soil the red soils cover over 66 percent of the area in the Reyalaseema districts. These types of soils have a low nutrient content. The black soils cover another 25 percent found in the Telengana region. The alluvial loamy clay soils found in Krishna and Godavari deltas cover 5 percent of the land. The coastal sands occupy 3 percent. The lacerate soils constituting 1 percent are seen in only in certain pockets.

Demographic features

Population

Andhra Pradesh is the fifth largest state in the Indian Union. It is the largest among the states in the southern region in terms of area and population. The state has registered a growth rate of 24.2 percent in population between 1981 and 1991. Which is slightly higher than the National growth rate by 2001 as it is 13.86 percent. For the first time in the last four decades the population growth rate of the state has overtaken according to the 2001 census Report. The population of Andhra Pradesh is 75,727,541 of which 55,223,944 resides in rural and 20,503,597 reside in urban areas. The urban population works out to 27.08 percent which the rural population out to 72.92 percent.[6]

Population Density

The population density of the state at 242 persons per sq. km. (1991) is lower than the national average (276) and much less than the density in the other southern states like Tamil Nadu and Kerala. However, it increased to 275 persons per sq. km in 2001 within the state the coastal Andhra region has a higher population density while Rayalaseema Region is sparsely populated. Sex ratio is defined as the number of females per thousand male populations. The sex ratio in Andhra Pradesh was showing decreasing trend since 1951 till 1991. However, for the first time, sex ratio has increased from 972 in 1991 to 978 in 2001. The sex ratio in Andhra Pradesh is higher than the all India figure, which is 933. However, the position of Andhra Pradesh is third among the four southern states i.e., after Kerala (1058) and Tamil Nadu (986). In Andhra Pradesh, the lowest sex ratio is registered in Rangareddy, Hyderabad and Anantapur, where as the highest sex ratio is registered in Nizamabad, Srikakulam and Vizianagaram. The female to male population ratio as per 1991 census is 972/1000 (1981=975/1000) as against the National Average of 927/1000. The sex ratio at all India level, according to 2001 census report, is 933, which is an improvement over the sex ratio of 927 at 1991.[7]

Literacy

The most important characteristic of population is literacy which is a pre-requisite for the over all development of the country, both socially and economically. The definition of "Literate" for census of India 2001 is the same as was adopted at 1991 census. A person is considered as literate if she/his is able to read and write with understanding in any language. One who can merely read but cannot write is not considered as literate. However, to qualify as a literate it is not necessary that a person should have received any formal education. As in 1991 census all the children below 7 years of age have been treated as illiterates during census of India-2001. The literacy rate of Andhra Pradesh works out to 61.11 at 2001 as against 44.09 in 1991. The literacy rate for rural India is 55.33 in 2001 as against 35.74 in 1991. The literacy rate for urban India is 76.39 in 2001 as against 66.35 in 1991.

In the State of Andhra Pradesh among the districts Hyderabad is at the top with a literacy rate of 79.04 percent followed by West Godavari with 73.95 percent, Krishna with 69.91 percent and Chittoor with 67.46 percent. The least literate district is Mahbubnagar with 45.53 percent followed by Vizianagaram with 51.82 percent and Medak with 50.24 percent. Among the rural population, West Godavari district ranks first in rural literacy rate with 72.48 percent followed by Krishna with 65.56 percent and Chittoor with 63.67 percent while least rural literacy was recorded in Mahbubnagar district with 46.86 percent (2001 Census Report).

Among the males, the literacy rate is 70.85 percent as against 51.17 percent among females as per 2001 census. Among the rural males the literacy rate is 66.13 percent as against 44.36 percent among the rural females. In totality, the literacy rate of

Andhra Pradesh is lower than the all India literacy rate and difference in literacy rate between rural and urban and between male and female is very wide (2001 Census Report).

Rural population

Revenue villages together with hamlets, if any, constitute the rural frame. There are 28,123 villages in Andhra Pradesh at 2001 as compared to 28,000 at 1991. The rural population accounts for 73.11 percent of the total population in the state as per 1991 census while the percentage of rural population is 72.92 percent as per 2001 census figures.

There is a steady decline in the rural population over the decades. As per 2001 census report, among the districts of Andhra Pradesh, Mahbubnagar ranks first with a rural population of 98.41 percent to the total population followed by Srikakulam with 89 percent and Nalgonda with 86.74 percent. Rangareddy district has the least rural population with the percentage of 46.73 percent.

In absolute numbers, the largest rural population is in the East Godavari District with 37,35,908 Guntur and Mahbubnagar districts with 31,74,288 and 31,35,445 follow it respectively. In absolute numbers, the lowest rural population is in Rangareddy district with 16,38,532 followed by Adilabad with 18,23,004 and Vizianagaram with 18,33,010.

Work force

Nearly two-thirds (69 percent) of the work force are engaged in agriculture. About 27.74 percent of the agricultural work force is cultivators and the agricultural labourers constitute 41 percent, which is much higher than the National average of 37.5 percent. Kerala is the only other state where the proportion of Agricultural labourers to total work force is higher than Andhra Pradesh at 67.8 percent. Of these engaged in non-agricultural activities one-third were engaged in manufacturing, another one-third in trade and transport and the rest in other pursuits. The proportion of female workers to total female population is 20 percent for Andhra Pradesh as against 15 percent for the country.

Characteristics of Andhra Pradesh Economy

Andhra Pradesh is one among the less developed states in the country as is evident from its relative position in respect of several indicators of economic performance and social services. Andhra Pradesh continues to be an agricultural state with 69 percent of its population dependent on agriculture.

Administrative Units

The state is divided into 23 districts and 7 zones.[8] The earlier development blocks, which were mostly coterminous with the revenue taluk boundaries were further sub-divided into Mandals by bifurcating each district was further sub-divided into 50-60 Mandals. Totally there are 1128 panchayat Mandals coterminous with the revenue Mandals created for the purpose of development and regulatory administration in the entire state by the end of March 2006.

The administrative head of each Panchayat Mandal is Mandal Development officer and the administrative head of each Revenue Mandal is Mandal Revenue officer till 2007 in which year earlier nomenclature of Tahsildar has been restored by the Government of Andhra Pradesh. Mandal President is the elected political head of the mandal area. The mandal is the hub of all development activity in the district. The Mandal Development office with his general and technical staff implements all the development schemes. Each mandal comprises of 15 to 25 villages for the purpose of administrative convenience. Each village has village secretariat headed by a village secretary who is also known as village executive officer. He is the administrative head of the village. The political head of each village is called sarpanch or president. In every village, Gram

Sabha is constituted consisting of all village voters. This institution facilitates the selection of participants for the development schemes. Gram Sabha is the micro-planning institution at the village level, which secures grassroots administration. Development strategies are coordinated through the Panchayati Raj Institutions (PRIs) with the active involvement of Non-Governmental Organisations (NGOs), Banks and the Line Departments of the Government of Andhra Pradesh. In East Godavari District there are more than 36 NGOs out of which 8 are actively involved in developmental and promotional function in the districts.

The Study Areas

A brief discussion of the profiles of the study areas i.e., Anantapur district, Warangal district and East Godawari district has been presented.

Profile of Anantapur District

Anantapur offers some vivid glimpses of the prehistoric past. It is generally held that the place got its name from 'Anaatasagaram', a big tank, which means "Endless Ocean". The villages of Anaantasagaram and Bukkarayasamudram were constructed by Chilkkavodeya, the minister of Bukka-I, a Vijayanagar ruler.[9] Some authorities assert that Anaantasagaram was named after Bukka's queen, while some contend that it must have been known after Anantarasa Chikkavodeya himself,[10] as Bukka had no queen by that name.

Anantapur is familiarly known as "Hande Anantapuram". 'Hande' means chief of the Vijayanagar period. Anantapur and a few other places were gifted by the Vijayanagar rulers to Hanumappa Naidu of the Hande family. The place subsequently came under the Qutub Shahis, Mughals, and the Nawabs of Cuddapah, although the Hande chiefs continued to rule as their subordinates. It was occupied by the Palergar of Bellary during the time of Ramappa but was eventually won back by his son, Siddappa. Morari Rao Ghorpade attacked Anantapur in 1757. Though the army resisted for some time, Siddappa ultimately bought off the enemy for Rs 50,000.

It then came into the possession of Hyder Ali and Tipu Sultan. Tipu hanged all the male members of the Siddappa family except Siddappa who escaped from his confinement at Srirangapatnam. After Tipu's death, it was once again taken back by Siddappa. Siddappa submitted himself to Nizam because of the treaty of 1799, who took the total control of the area. He was later pensioned off when British occupied the territory Anantapur District was formed in the year 1882 having been separated from Bellary District.

Later on, it was expanded with the addition of Revenue Mandals of Kadiri, Mudigubba, Nallamada, N.P. Kunta, Talupula, Nallacheruvu, O.D. Cheruvu, Tanakal, Amadagur and Gandlapenta (previous Kadiri Taluk) from Cuddapah District in the year 1910. During the year 1956, the present Revenue Mandals of Rayadurg, D. Hirehal, Kanekal, Bommanahal and Gummagatta of Bellary District were added to Anantapur District. The District has been divided into 3 Revenue Divisions consisting of 63 Revenue Mandals (Anantapur Division 20, Dharmavaram Division 17 and Penukonda Division 26).

Soil

The soils in Anantapur District are predominantly red except Kanekal, Bommanahal, Vidapanakal, Uravakonda, Vajrakarur, Guntakal, Gooty, Pamidi, Peddavadugur, Yadiki, Tadipatri, Yellanur, Peddapappur and Putlur Mandals. In these Mandals red and black soils occur almost in equal proportion. Thus, 76% red soils, 24% are black soils.

Population

There are 929 inhabited villages, out of 964 total Revenue

villages of the District. The number of villages in size group of 500 to 1999 forms 36.71% of the total inhabited villages. The size group of 2000 to 4999 forms 38.64% and the size group of 5000 to 9999 forms 12.81% only out of total villages, while 84 villages (9.04%) of total inhabited villages are having population less than 500. There are 26 villages with more than 10000 population excluding Towns.

Profile of Warangal

Warangal also known as Orugallu, and Ekasila Nagaram) is a city and a municipal corporation in Warangal district in the Indian State of Andhra Pradesh.[11] Warangal is located 148 kilometers (92 mi) northeast of the state capital of Hyderabad and is the administrative headquarters of Warangal District. This district is a combination of three cities: Warangal, Hanamakonda and Kazipet. It has a population of nearly 1 million including Hanamakonda and Kazipet.[12]

Geography and Climate

Warangal is located at 18.0°N 79.58°E. It has an average elevation of 302 meters (990 feet).

Located in the semi-arid Telangana region of Andhra Pradesh, Warangal has a predominantly hot and dry climate. Summers start in March, and peak in May with average high temperatures in the 42°C (108°F) range. The monsoon arrives in June and lasts until September with about 550 mm (22 in) of precipitation. A dry, mild winter starts in late November and lasts until early February. With little humidity and average temperatures in the 22–23°C (72–73°F) range, this is the best time to visit Warangal.

Governance

Warangal city is the headquarters of Warangal district. Warangal district contributes a total of twelve seats (city has two; that of Warangal East and Warangal West) in the lower house of the State Legislature and two seats (Warangal and Mahabubabad) in lower house of Indian Parliament.

Census

As of 2011 India census,[3] Warangal had a population of 759,594. Males constitute 51% of the population and females 49%. Warangal has an average literacy rate of 84.16%, higher than the national average of 74.04%: male literacy is 91.54%, and female literacy is 76.79%. In Warangal, 11% of the population is under 6 years of age.

Education

Warangal has educational institutions such as National Institute of Technology, Warangal and Kakatiya Medical College. Established in 1959 as the first of Regional Engineering Colleges in the country, the NIT grew into an important national level institute for engineering studies.

- National Institute of Technology, Warangal (formerly known as Regional Engineering College)
- Kakatiya University
- Kakatiya Medical College
- Kakatiya Institute of Technology and Science (KITS)[4]

There are several non-governmental organisations active in primary and secondary education in Warangal District. Of these, the best known are KITS, WITS, Rural Development Foundation and Institute for Technology and Management, Warangal (ITM Warangal).

East Godavari

East Godavari District (often abbreviated as E.G. Dist, E.G. Dt) is a district situated on the northeast of the state of Andhra Pradesh in India. Its district headquarters is Kakinada. It is the second richest district in the whole country. This district was formed in 1925 when old Godavari district was divided into west and east districts. In 1959, Bhadrachalam Revenue Division consisting of Bhadrachalam and Nuguru Venkatapuram Taluks of East Godavari district, which were on the other side of the river Godavari were merged into Khammam district on grounds of geographical contiguity and administrative viability. The district is bounded on the north by Visakhapatnam District, on the northwest by Khammam District, on the east and south by the Bay of Bengal and on the west by West Godavari District. The small enclave [12 sq mi (30 km^2)] of the Yanam district of Pondicherry state lies within this district. Kakinada and Rajahmundry are the two large cities in the Godavari districts. Kakinada is an educational hub and a rapid growing city in Coastal Andhra in industrial sector. Rajahmundry is one of the well known business centres in Coastal Andhra.

The District is known as rice bowl of Andhra Pradesh with lush paddy fields and coconut groves. It is also known as another Kerala. East Godavari is the Rice Granary of Andhra Pradesh, it beckons tourists to have a glimpse of its rich cultural heritage.

It is the most populous district of Andhra Pradesh (out of 23).[13]

After India's independence in 1947, the former Madras Presidency of British India became India's Madras State. In 1953, the northern districts of Madras state, including Godavari District, became the new state of Andhra Pradesh. Yanam was relinquished by the French in 1954, but one condition of the cession treaty was the retention of the district's separate and distinct identity, which also applied to the other South Indian enclaves constituting today's Pondicherry state.

Geography and Climate

East Godavari district occupies an area of 10,807 square kilometres (4,173 sq mi)[14] comparatively equivalent to

Indonesia's Sumba Island.[15] The district has hilly terrain to the west and plains to the east. To the east of the district lies the Bay of Bengal. The district Headquarters Kakinada lies on the coast. The district receives rainfall from June to October; both southwest and northeast monsoon contribute to the rainfall. Average rainfall varies widely from 100 centimeters at the northern part of the coast to 140 centimeters at the extreme western parts of the hills.

Demographics

According to the 2011 census East Godavari district has a population of 5,151,549 roughly equal to the United Arab Emirates[16] or the US state of Colorado.[17] This gives it a ranking of 19th in India (out of a total of 640) and 2nd in its state. The district has a population density of 477 inhabitants per square kilometer (1,240 /sq mi). Its population growth rate over the decade 2001-2011 was 5.1%. East Godavari has a sex ratio of 1005 females for every 1000 males, and a literacy rate of 71.35%.

East Godavari district has a total population of 5,151,549 of which male and female were 2,569,419 and 2,582,130 respectively. There was change of 5.10 percent in the population compared to population as per 2001 census. The census data suggest a density of 477 in 2011 compared to 454 of 2001.

Average literacy rate of East Godavari in 2011 were 71.35 compared to 65.48 of 2001. If things are looked out at gender-wise, male and female literacy were 74.91 and 67.82 respectively.

With regards to Sex Ratio in East Godavari, it stood at 1005 per 1000 male compared to 2001 census figure of 993. The average national sex ratio in India is 940 as per latest reports of Census 2011 Directorate.

There were total 492,446 children under age of 0-6 against 613,490 of 2001 census. Of total 492,446 male and female were 250,086 and 242,360 respectively. Child Sex Ratio as per census

2011 was 969 compared to 978 of census 2001. In 2011, Children under 0-6 formed 9.56 percent of East Godavari District compared to 12.52 percent of 2001.

Working of PRIs in Andhra Pradesh

In this part a brief presentation regarding the working of PRIs in Andhra Pradesh, the caste compassion has been analyzed.

Table 4.1: District, Gram Panchayat-wise Distribution in Andhra Pradesh

Sl. No.	District	No. of Village Panchayats
1.	Adilabad	866
2.	Anantapur	1001
3.	Chittoor	1381
4.	East Godavari	1012
5.	Guntur	1016
6.	Karimnagar	1194
7.	Khammam	771
8.	Krishna	972
9.	Kurnool	899
10.	Mahbubnagar	1348
11.	Medak	1109
12.	Nalgonda	1178
13.	Nizamabad	718
14.	Prakasam	1036
15.	Rangareddi	705
16.	SPSR Nellore	961
17.	Srikakulam	1101
18.	Visakhapatanam	944
19.	Vizianagaram	929
20.	Warangal	1014
21.	West Godavari	888
22.	Y.S.R.	800
	TOTAL	21843

Compiled from the data collected from Official Documents of Panchayat Raj and Rural Development, Andhra Pradesh.

Table 4.1 discusses the district and gram panchayat-wise distribution in Andhra Pradesh. The table shows that the

Andhra Pradesh has been divided into three division i.e., old Andhra, which consists of 9 districts. Among these there are highest number of Mandals in East Godavari and the lowest number i.e., 34 in Srikakulam district. As regards to gram

Table 4.2: Caste-wise Distribution of Population in Three Regions

S. No.	Caste Name	Population	Percentage
	Total		100%
	Forward Castes:		33%
01.	Reddy		6.3%
02.	Kamma		4.7%
03.	Kapu		15%
04.	Velama		3%
05.	Vysya		2.6%
06.	Kshatriya		1.1%
07.	Brahmin		
	Scheduled Castes:		**17.5%**
01.	Mala		10%
02.	Madiga		7.5%
	Minorities:		**7.5%**
01.	Muslims		
02.	Christians		
	Backward Castes		**42%**
01.	Yadav		6.4%
02.	Telaga		5.3%
03.	Chakali		4.3%
04.	Mutarasi		3.4%
05.	Balija		3.2%
06.	Kummari		3%
07.	Devangana		2.2%
08.	Goundla		2.1%
09.	Vaddera		2%
10.	Mangali		1.4%
11.	Kuruma		1.4%
12.	Idiga		1.1%
13.	Kummari		1%
14.	Munnuru Kapu		0.9%
15.	Boya		0.9%
16.	Besta		0.8%
17.	Uppara		0.5%
18.	Gavara		0.5%
19.	Jangama		0.5%

Source: Compiled from the data collected from Official Documents of Panchayatraj and Rural Development, Andhra Pradesh.

panchayat the highest number i.e., 1101 are in Sirthuthklare and the lowest number 888 are in West Godavari district.

In Rayalaseema there are four districts, among these 66, the highest number of Mandals are Chittoor district and the lowest 50 Mandals are in Kadapa district. In Rayalaseema, 1381 the highest members of gram panchayats are in Chittoor district and the lowest number 800 are in Kadapa district.

In Telangana there are 10 districts, among these the highest number i.e., 64 Mandals are in Mahbubnagar district, and the lowest number 33 members are in Rangareddy district. As regards to gram panchayats, 1348 the highest number are in Mahbubnagar district and the lowest 705 are in Rangareddy district.

Table 4.2 discusses the caste-wise distribution of population in three regions. The table reveals that the forward castes consist of 33%, scheduled castes are 17.5%, minorities are 75% and the highest percentage i.e., 42% is from backward castes. Among the backward castes the highest percentage is from Yadava (6.4%) followed by Telaga (5.3%), Chalhali (4.3%) and the lowest percentage is from Uppara, Gavara and Jangam (0.5%) respectively.

Table 4.3 discusses that the castes, district-wise distribution of Zilla Praja Parishad members in Andhra region. The table reveals that there are more number of Zilla Praja Parishad members in Prakaem Zilla Praja Parishad i.e., 32 out of 56. Followed by 24 members out of 52 in Adilabad district. The lowest number i.e., 18 members out of 63 are in Anantapur district from Rayalaseema region.

The over all findings of the table is that inspite of the majority of people belonging to backward castes there exists large number of Zilla Praja Parishad members in Anantapur district. It is observed that the factionalism and the domination of upper castes are predominant in the working of zilla panchayat in Anantapur district.

Table 4.3: Backward Caste-wise Distribution of ZP members in Andhra Pradesh

S. No.	District	Backward Castes	Total
1.	Adilabad	24	52
2.	Anantapur	18	63
3.	Chittoor	23	65
4.	East Godavari	20	58
5.	Guntur	12	57
6.	Kadapa		50
7.	Karimnagar	17	57
8.	Khammam		46
9.	Krishna		49
10.	Kurnool	23	53
11.	Mahaboobnagar		46
12.	Medak	22	46
13.	Nalgonda	15	59
14.	Nellore	14	46
15.	Nizamabad		36
16.	Prakasam	32	56
17.	Ranga Reddy		33
18.	Srikakulam	19	38
19.	Visakhapatnam		39
20.	Vizianagaram		34
21.	Warangal	16	50
22.	West Godavari	13	46
		268	**1079**

Source: Compiled from the data collected from Official Documents of Panchayat Raj and Rural Development, Andhra Pradesh.

Table 4.4 discusses district-wise and Sex-wise distribution of Zilla Praja Parishad members in Andhra Pradesh. The table observed that among the male members, there are highest number in Mahbubnagar district and Chittoor i.e., 41 and 40 respectively. The lowest number of male member i.e., 20 are from Vijayanagar district. As far as concerning of female members, the highest number of 25 members are in Anantapur and Chittoor district and the lowest number 12 members are in Medak district.

Table 4.4: Sex-wise Distribution of ZP members in Andhra Pradesh

S. No	District	Male	Female	Total
1.	Adilabad	35	17	
2.	Anantapur	38	25	
3.	Chittoor	40	25	
4.	East Godavari	38	20	
5.	Guntur	23	24	
6.	Kadapa	32	18	
7.	Karimnagar	37	20	
8.	Khammam	27	19	
9.	Krishna	31	18	
10.	Kurnool	36	17	
11.	Mahbubnagar	41	23	
12.	Medak	32	12	
13.	Nalgonda	38	21	
14.	Nellore	24	22	46
15.	Nizamabad	23	13	
16.	Prakasam	35	21	
17.	Ranga Reddy	21	12	
18.	Srikakulam	23	15	
19.	Visakhapatnam	20	19	39
20.	Vizianagaram	20	14	34
21.	Warangal	28	22	
22.	West Godavari	29	17	

Source: Compiled from the data collected from Official Documents of Panchayat Raj and Rural Development, Andhra Pradesh.

Table 4.5: Sex-wise distribution of chairman of Zilla Praja Parishad in Andhra Pradesh

S. No.	District	Male	Female	Total
1.	Adilabad		01	01
2.	Anantapur	01		01
3.	Chittoor	01		01
4.	East Godavari	01		01
5.	Guntur	01		01
6.	Kadapa	01		01
7.	Karimnagar		01	01
8.	Khammam		01	01
9.	Krishna	01		01
10.	Kurnool	01		01
11.	Mahbubnagar	01		01
12.	Medak	01		01
13.	Nalgonda	01		01

(*Contd...*)

14.	Nellore	01		01
15.	Nizamabad		01	01
16.	Prakasam		01	01
17.	Ranga Reddy		01	01
18.	Prakasam		01	01
19.	Srikakulam	01		01
20.	Visakhapatnam	01		01
21.	Vizianagaram		01	01
22.	Warangal		01	01
23.				01
24.				01

Source: Compiled from the data collected from Official Documents of Panchayat Raj and Rural Development, Andhra Pradesh.

Table 4.5 discusses Sex-wise distribution of chairman of Zilla Praja Parishad in Andhra Pradesh. The table reveals that out of the total 9 chairman's are from women.

Table 4.6: Sex-wise Distribution of MPP Chairman in Andhra Pradesh

S. No	District	Male	Female	Total
1.	Adilabad	23	32	55
2.	Anantapur	28	35	63
3.	Chittoor	28	39	37
4.	East Godavari	23	35	58
5.	Guntur	21	39	57
6.	Kadapa	20	29	49
7.	Karimnagar	27	31	58
8.	Khammam	19	27	46
9.	Krishna	24	26	50
10.	Kurnool	21	32	53
11.	Mahbubnagar	28	35	63
12.	Medak	20	26	46
13.	Nalgonda	18	30	48
14.	Nellore	20	24	46
15.	Nizamabad	18	18	36
16.	Prakasam	21	30	51
17.	Ranga Reddy	13	20	51
18.	Srikakulam	17	21	38
19.	Visakhapatnam	14	25	39
20.	Vizianagaram	17	17	34
21.	Warangal	20	30	50
22.	West Godavari	21	29	50

Source: Compiled from the data collected from Official Documents of Panchayat Raj and Rural Development, Andhra Pradesh.

Table 4.6 discusses sex-wise distribution of MPP chairman in Andhra Pradesh. The table reveals that among the male members, the highest number 28 members are from Anantapur and Chittoor districts. Among the female members the highest number 39 members are in Chittoor district followed by 35 members in Anantapur and Godavari respectively.

Table 4.7: Castes-wise Distribution of MPPS in Andhra Pradesh

S. No.	District	Total	BCs	Percentage
1.	Adilabad	55	28	50.90
2.	Anantapur	63	28	44.44
3.	Chittoor	67	34	50.74
4.	East Godavari	56	26	46.43
5.	Guntur	57	23	40.35
6.	Karimnagar	58	34	58.62
7.	Khammam	46	14	30.43
8.	Krishna	50	14	28.00
9.	Kurnool	53	21	39.62
10.	Mahbubnagar	63	21	33.33
11.	Medak	46	22	47.83
12.	Nalgonda	48	17	35.42
13.	Nizamabad	36	19	52.78
14.	Prakasam	51	19	37.25
15.	Rangareddi	33	17	51.52
16.	Nellore	46	16	34.78
17.	Srikakulam	38	34	89.47
18.	Visakhapatanam	39	17	43.59
19.	Vizianagaram	34	28	82.35
20.	Warangal	50	31	62.00
21.	West Godavari	50	26	52.00
22.	Y.S.R.	49	35	71.43
23.	Total	1088	524	

Source: Compiled from the data collected from Official Documents of Panchayat Raj and Rural Development, Andhra Pradesh.

Table 4.7 discusses caste-wise distribution of MPPs in Andhra Pradesh. The table reveals that out of 488 MPPs, there are 524 MPPs belonging to various categories of backward castes. Among the backward castes the highest percentage (71.43%) of backward castes are from YSR district, followed by 89.47% from

Srikakulam. The lowest percentage 2800 of backward castes are from Krishna district.

Table 4.8: District-wise, Number-wise Distribution of Gram Panchayats in Andhra Pradesh

Sl. No.	District	No. of Village Panchayats
1.	Adilabad	866
2.	Anantapur	1001
3.	Chittoor	1381
4.	East Godavari	1012
5.	Guntur	1016
6.	Karimnagar	1194
7.	Khammam	771
8.	Krishna	972
9.	Kurnool	899
10.	Mahbubnagar	1348
11.	Medak	1109
12.	Nalgonda	1178
13.	Nizamabad	718
14.	Prakasam	1036
15.	Rangareddi	705
16.	SPSR Nellore	961
17.	Srikakulam	1101
18.	Visakhapatanam	944
19.	Vizianagaram	929
20.	Warangal	1014
21.	West Godavari	888
22.	Y.S.R.	800
	TOTAL	**21843**

Source: Compiled from the data collected from Official Documents of Panchayat Raj and Rural Development, Andhra Pradesh.

Table 4.8 discusses district-wise distribution of gram panchayats in Andhra Pradesh. The table reveals that in Andhra Pradesh there are 21843 gram panchayat in total. Out of which, the highest number 1381 gram panchayats are in Chittoor district followed by 1348 gram panchayat in Mahbubnagar district. The lowest number i.e., 705 gram panchayat are in Rangareddy district.

Table 4.9: Sex-wise Distribution of Sarpanchs in Andhra Pradesh

S. No.	District	Male	Female	Total
1.	Adilabad	290	576	866
2.	Anantapur	489	512	1001
3.	Chittoor	427	954	1381
4.	East Godavari	457	555	1012
5.	Guntur	328	688	1016
6.	Karimnagar	351	843	1194
7.	Khammam	201	570	771
8.	Krishna	259	713	972
9.	Kurnool	264	635	899
10.	Mahbubnagar	425	923	1348
11.	Medak	328	781	1109
12.	Nalgonda	299	879	1178
13.	Nizamabad	245	473	718
14.	Prakasam	356	680	1036
15.	Rangareddi	289	416	705
16.	SPSR Nellore	322	639	961
17.	Srikakulam	356	745	1101
18.	Visakhapatanam	298	646	944
19.	Vizianagaram	289	640	929
20.	Warangal	302	712	1014
21.	West Godavari	337	551	888
22.	Y.S.R.	314	486	800
23.	Total	7226	14617	21843

Compiled from the data collected from Official Documents of Panchayat Raj and Rural Development, Andhra Pradesh.

Table 4.9 discusses the sex-wise distribution of sarpanchs in Andhra Pradesh. The table reveals that out of the total of 21843, the male sarpanchs are 7226 and female sarpanchs are 14617 respectively.

References

1. "Census of India". *Census of India 2001*. Government of India. 27 May 2002. Archived from the original on 3 April 2007. Retrieved 14 April 2007.
2. "Citizen Help". AP Online. 1 November 1956. Archived from the original on 4 April 2009. Retrieved 3 March 2009.

3. Aptdc, Andhra Pradesh Tourism Development Corporation (27 May 2010). "APTDC–Andhra Pradesh Tourism Development Corporation". Tourisminap.com. Archived from the original on 6 August 2010. Retrieved 15 August 2010.
4. August 2012. http://www.thehindu.com/sci-tech/energy-and-environment/article3719048.ece?homepage=true.
5. "Andhra Pradesh Geography". Maharashtraweb.com.Archived from the original on 29 September 2010. Retrieved 15 August 2010.
6. "Distribution of 10,000 Persons by Language — India, States and Union Territories 2001". Office of the Registrar General & Census Commissioner, India. 2001. Retrieved 16 June 2010.
7. "Human Development Report 2007". A P online.gov.in.Archived from the original on 19 September 2010. Retrieved
8. "History of Andhra Pradesh". Government of Andhra Pradesh. 2002. Retrieved 22 July 2012.
9. Government of Andhra Pradesh, District Gazetteers, Anantapur, 1970, Chapter I, pp. 1-2.
10. Epigraphically Reports of 1906 and Epigraphica Carnatica Vol. X.
11. "World Gazetteer — Population of Warangal".
12. http://censusindia.gov.in/towns/ap_towns.pdf Census India - Warangal
13. "District Census 2011". Census2011.co.in. 2011. Retrieved 2011-09-30.
14. Srivastava, Dayawanti et al. (ed.) (2010). "States and Union Territories: Andhra Pradesh: Government". *India 2010: A Reference Annual* (54th ed.). New Delhi, India: Additional Director General, Publications Division, Ministry of Information and Broadcasting (India), Government of India. pp. 1111–1112. ISBN 978-81-230-1617-7.
15. "Island Directory Tables: Islands by Land Area". United Nations Environment Program. 1998-02-18. Retrieved 2011-10-11. "Sumba 10,711"
16. US Directorate of Intelligence. "Country Comparison: Population". Retrieved 2011-10-01. "United Arab Emirates 5,148,664."
17. "2010 Resident Population Data". U. S. Census Bureau. Retrieved 2011-09-30. "Colorado 5,029,196."

Chapter – V

Socio – Economic Background of the Respondents

In this chapter the political participation of backward castes in the institutions of panchayat raj has been analyzed on the basis of field experience. The field evidence with reference to the working of backward castes has been collected from the three districts i.e., Anantapur from Rayalaseema, Warangal from Telangana and East Godawari from Andhra Region and thus the collected data has been transformed in to computer and the respective tables are generated.

Table 5.1: District-wise Distribution of Respondents in Andhra Pradesh

S. No	District	Frequency	Percentage
1.	Anantapur	150	33.33
2.	Warangal	150	33.33
3.	West Godavari	150	33.33
4.	Total	450	100.00

Source: Compiled from the data collected from field work.[1]

Table 5.1 shows the district-wise distribution of sample respondents in the study area. It is observed from the table that the respondents have drawn from three district i.e., Anantapur district from Rayalaseema, Warangal from Telangana and West Godvari from Andhra region. The total respondents are 450, out of which 150 from each district.

Table 5.2: Nature of Respondents

S. No	District	Frequency	Percentage
1.	Chairman/Vice-Chairman	03	0.67
2.	President MPP	24	5.33
3.	Chair Persons Village Panchayat	45	10.00
4.	Z P Members	60	13.33
5.	MPTC Members	60	13.33
6.	Village Panchayat Members	90	20.00
7.	General Public	160	35.56
8.	Total	450	100.00

Source: Compiled from the data collected from field work.

Table 4.2 discusses the nature/type of members in the institutions of panchayat raj-wise distribution. The table reveals that the respondents' consists of chairman and vice-chairman are 3 with 0.67%, presidents of MPP are 24 with 5.33%, chairpersons of village panchayats are 45 with 10%, members of zilla panchayat are 60 with 13.33%, MPTC member are 60 with 13.33%, village panchayat members are 90 with 20% and the general public are 160 with 35.56%.

Table 5.3: Caste-wise Distribution of Respondents

S. No	Caste	Frequency	Percentage
1.	Cat-A	125	27.78
2.	Cat-B	135	30.00
3.	Cat-C	90	20.00
4.	Cat-D	100	22.22
5.	Total	450	100.00

Source: Compiled from the data collected from field work.[3]

Table 5.3 discusses the caste-wise distribution of respondents in the study area. The table reveals that the respondents belonging to category 'A' are 125 with 27.78%, from category 'B' are 135 with 30%, from category 'C' are 90 with 20% and from category 'D' are 100 with 22.22%.

The over all observation is that the higher social categorical among backward castes are more in the institutions of panchayat raj in Andhra Pradesh.

Table 5.4: Age-wise Distribution of Respondents

S. No	Age	Frequency	Percentage
1.	18-25	116	25.78
2.	26-35	267	59.33
3.	36-45	59	13.11
4.	46-& Above	8	1.78
5.	Total	450	100.00

Source: Compiled from the data collected from field work.[4]

Table 5.4 discusses the age-wise distribution of respondents. It is observed from the table that out of the total 450 respondents, the highest number 267 with 59.33% of respondents are from the age group of 26-35, followed by 116 respondents with 25.78% are from the age group of 18-25, 59 respondents with 13.11% are from the age group of 36-45 and the lowest number of respondents with 1.78% are from the age group of 46 and above.

The over all observation of the table is that there exists more number of respondents and representatives belonging to younger and middle age group.

Table 5.5: Gender-wise Distribution of Respondents

S. No	Gender	Frequency	Percentage
1.	Male	260	57.78
2.	Female	190	42.22
3.	Total	450	100.00

Source: Compiled from the data collected from field work.[5]

Table 5.5 discusses the gender-wise distribution of respondents in the study area. It is observed from the table that out of the total 450, the male respondents are 260 with 57.78% and the lowest respondents are 190 with 42.22%.

It is observed that the female respondents are more than 30 percentage.

Table 5.6: Marital Status-wise Distribution of Respondents

S. No	Marital Status	Frequency	Percentage
1.	Unmarried	59	13.11
2.	Married	324	72.00
3.	Widow/Widower	39	8.67
4.	Divorced	28	6.22
5.	Total	450	100.00

Source: Compiled from the data collected from field work.[6]

Table 5.6 discusses the marital status-wise distribution of respondents in the study area. The table shows that out of the total 450 respondents, the highest number 324 respondents with 72% are married, followed by 359 respondents with 13.11% are unmarried, 39 respondents with 8.67% are widows and the lowest number 28 respondents with 6.22% are divorced from their husbands.

It is observed from the table that even unmarried and divorced women are also participating in the working of PRIs in the study area.

Table 5.7: Religion-wise Distribution of Respondents

S. No	Religion	Frequency	Percentage
1.	Hindu	358	79.56
2.	Christian	58	12.89
3.	Others	34	7.56
4.	Total	450	100.00

Source: Compiled from the data collected from field work.[7]

Table 5.7 discusses the religion-wise distribution of respondents in the study area. It is observed from the table that out of the total 450 respondents, the highest number 358 respondents with 79.56% are from Hindus, followed by 58 respondents with 12.89% are from Christians and 34 respondents with 7.56% are from other religion.

The over all observation of the table is that the respondents are from the many religions background.

Table 5.8: Educational Status-wise Distribution of Respondents

S. No	Education	Frequency	Percentage
1.	Illiterates	68	15.11
2.	Up to 10th	139	30.89
3.	PUC	112	24.89
4.	Graduates	87	19.33
5.	Others	44	9.78
6.	Total	450	100.00

Source: Compiled from the data collected from field work.[8]

Table 5.8 discusses the educational status-wise distribution of respondents in the study area. The table shows that the respondents are from both illiterates and educated. 68 respondents with 15.11 percent are illiterates, 139 respondents with 30.89% are from 1st standard to 10th standard, 112 respondents with 24.89% have studied upto PUC, 87 respondents with 19.33% are graduates and 44 respondents with 9.78% having other educational qualifications such as Master degree, technical education and other diplomas.

It is observed from the table that nearly 85% of respondents are educated.

Table 5.9: Occupation-wise Distribution of Respondents

S. No	Occupation	Frequency	Percentage
1.	Agriculture	213	47.33
2.	Cooli	87	19.33
3.	Business	48	10.67
4.	Artisans	37	8.22
5.	Others	65	14.44
6.	Total	450	100.00

Source: Compiled from the data collected from field work.

Table 5.9 discusses the occupation-wise distribution of respondents in the study area. The occupation of the respondents reveals the economic status and their commitment in the working of PRIS. The table shows that out of the total 450, the highest number 213 respondents with 47.33% are from agricultural background, followed by 87 respondent with

19.33% are from cooli or labour background. 48 respondents with 10.67% are from business, 37 respondents with 8.22% are from agricultural such as supportive class to agriculture families and 65 respondents with 14.44% are from other occupational backgrounds.

The over all observation of the table is that, majority of respondents, 300 with 68.66 are from agriculture and cooli background.

Table 5.10: Family Income-wise Distribution of Respondents

S. No	Income	Frequency	Percentage
1.	5000-40,000	289	64.22
2.	10,001 – 20,000	112	24.89
3.	20,0001- 30,000	87	19.33
4.	30.001 & Above	38	8.44
5.	Total	450	100.00

Source: Compiled from the data collected from field work.

Table 5.10 discusses the family income-wise distribution of respondents in the study area. The table shows that out of the total, the highest number 289 respondents with 64.22% are from the income range of Rs 50000 – 10000, followed by 112 respondents with 24.89% are from the income range of Rs 10,001 to 20,000. And the lowest number 38 respondents with 8.44% are from the income range of Rs 30001 and above.

It is observed from the table that there exists more number of respondents with less income and the less number of respondents with higher range of income.

Table 5.11: Family Size-wise Distribution of Respondents

S. No	Size of the Family	Frequency	Percentage
1.	Two Members	48	10.67
2.	Three Members	142	31.56
3.	Four Members	189	42.00
4.	Above Members	71	15.78
5.	Total	450	100.00

Source: Compiled from the data collected from field work.

Table 5.11 discusses the family size-wise distribution of respondents. It is observed from the table that out of the total 450, the highest number 189 respondents with 42% are from the families of more than four members, followed by 142 respondents with 31.56% are from the family having three members. The lowest number 48 with 10.67% of respondents are from the families of two members.

Table 5.12: Land Size-wise Distribution of Respondents

S. No	Size of the Family	Frequency	Percentage
1.	< 5 Acres	154	34.22
2.	5-10 Acers	207	46.00
3.	11-15 Acers	34	7.56
4.	No Land	55	12.22
5.	Total	450	100.00

Source: Compiled from the data collected from field work.

Table 5.12 discusses the land size-wise distribution of respondents. It is observed from the table that the highest number 207 numbers with 56% of the respondents are in positions of 5 to 10 acres, followed by 154 respondents with 34.22% are in positions of less than 5 acres of land.

It is observed from the table that people with less number of acres of land and with low economic status only are participating in the working of panchayat raj institutions in the study area.

Table 5.13: Source of the Irrigation of the Family-wise Distribution of Respondents

S. No	Source of Irrigation	Frequency	Percentage
1.	Mota	11	2.44
2.	Oil Engine	6	1.33
3.	Tank	18	4.00
4.	Depend on Rain	28	6.22
5.	Well	87	19.33
6.	Electric Motor	39	8.67
7.	No Land	237	52.67
8.	Total	450	100.00

Source: Compiled from the data collected from field work.

Table 5.13 discusses the sources of the irrigation of the family-wise distribution of respondents in the study area. The table reveals that 39 respondents with 19.67% have electric motors as source of irrigation, 87 respondents with 18.33% are in the position of well as source of irrigation.

It is observed from the table that majority of the respondents in the study area are depending on traditional modes of irrigation.

References

1. Compiled from data collected from field work regarding to district information.
2. Compiled from data collected from field work regarding to the information of nature of respondents.
3. Compiled from data collected from field work regarding to the information of Caste.
4. Compiled from data collected from field work regarding to the information of age.
5. Compiled from data collected from field work regarding to the information of gender.
6. Compiled from data collected from field work regarding to the information of martial status.
7. Compiled from data collected from field work regarding to the information of religion.
8. Compiled from data collected from field work regarding to the information of educational status.
9. Compiled from data collected from field work regarding to the information of occupational status.
10. Compiled from data collected from field work regarding to the information of family income.
11. Compiled from data collected from field work regarding to the information of family size.
12. Compiled from data collected from field work regarding to the information of land size.
13. Compiled from data collected from field work regarding to the information of source of irrigation.

Chapter – VI

Perception and Problems of Political Participation

It is widely believed that the analysis of age, education, caste, family structure, occupation, income, land holding, party affiliation, etc., are important in determining the nature of leadership. The data relating to socio-economic background of elected respondents of Panchayati Raj institutions were collected in the % study to get an insight into the emerging pattern of rural leadership in Anantapur, Warangal and East Godawari districts of Andhra Pradesh.

The socio-economic conditions play an important role in characterising the social life and behaviour of an individual. The socio-economic status of an individual affects the patterns of interaction in the society. It is therefore, essential to analyze the socio-economic background of the relationship between the leader and the environment. In a developing society like ours where forces of caste and kinship influence the social life and acute disparity in the standard of living and sub-culture among various groups and regions are existing[1], a study of the socio-economic conditions of OBC respondents would help reveal sociologically significant dimensions.

The socio-economic, educational and political background of the leaders would also enable us to anticipate as to what they are capable of doing, what we should expect from them and how well they are equipped to discharge the responsibilities developed upon them by the electorate[2].

Knowledge of socio-economic background of a community is an indispensable prerequisite, for the understanding of the thought or behaviours of its members. This holds good for all human communities, and more so in the case of SC/ST and OBC communities, which are intrinsically more traditional in their structure. As Geraint Parry observes: 'It is a widespread assumption of political sociology that social background and upbringing of a decision-maker will influence his attitudes and policies.[3]

Table 6.1 discusses the caste-wise distribution of opinion toward the purpose of panchayat raj institutions. The opinion of backward caste in Rayalaseema shows that out of the total 62 belonging to category 'A' (62.90%) of the respondents are aware of the panchayat raj institutions. Followed by 66.67% belonging to category 'B', (53.06%) of respondents belonging to the category 'C' and 62.16% of respondents belonging to Category 'D'. And at the same time the highest number with 66.67% of respondents belonging to category 'B' are not aware of panchayat raj institutions.

In Rayalaseema, the most backward caste i.e., category 'A' and 'B' are participating in panchayat raj institutions.

The caste-wise opinion in Telangana reveals that the majority of the respondents belonging to category 'B' are participating in panchayat raj institutions. The majority of respondents i.e. 19 each from category 'A' and 'B' are not aware of the working of PRIs.

In the developed region of Andhra Pradesh, i.e., Andhra region, 29 respondents belonging to category 'B' and 22 respondents belonging to category 'D' are participating in PRIs. The table reveals that majority of respondents i.e., 16 belonging to category 'A' are not participating in the activities of PRIs.

The observation of the table is that among the backward castes, category 'A' and 'B' are more in Rayalaseema. Category

Table 6.1: Caste-wise Distribution of Opinion toward the Purpose of Panchayat Raj Institutions

		Rayala Seema Backward Caste				Telangana Backward Caste				Andhra Backward Caste			
		A	B	C	D	A	B	C	D	A	B	C	D
S. No	Opinion	Frequ ency	Frequ-ency	Frequ-ency	Frequ-ency	Frequ-ency	Frequ-ency	Frequ-ency	Frequ-ency	Frequ-ency	Frequ-ency	Frequ-ency	Frequ-ency
1.	Yes	39 (62.90)	36 (66.67)	26 (53.06)	23 (62.16)	18 (48.65)	26 (63.41)	7 (28.00)	16 (64.00)	10 (38.46)	29 (72.50)	13 (81.25)	22 (57.89)
2.	No	23 (37.10)	19 (66.67)	23 (53.06)	14 (37.84)	19 (51.35)	19 (46.34)	5 (20.00)	10 (40.00)	16 (61.54)	6 (15.00)	6 (37.5)	15 (39.47)
3.	Total	62 (100.00)	54 (100.00)	49 (100.00)	37 (100.00)	37 (100.00)	41 (100.00)	25 (100.00)	25 (100.00)	26 (100.00)	40 (100.00)	16 (100.00)	38 (100.00)

Source: Compiled from the data collected from field work.

Table 6.2: Caste-wise and Region-wise Distribution of Opinion towards Attending the Grama Sabha

		Rayala Seema Backward Caste				Telangana Backward Caste				Andhra Backward Caste			
		A	B	C	D	A	B	C	D	A	B	C	D
S. No	Opinion	Frequ ency	Frequ-ency	Frequ-ency	Frequ-ency	Frequ-ency	Frequ-ency	Frequ-ency	Frequ-ency	Frequ-ency	Frequ-ency	Frequ-ency	Frequ-ency
1.	Yes	38 (61.29)	30 (55.56)	21 (42.86)	25 (67.57)	16 (43.24)	21 (51.22)	17 (68.00)	14 (56.00)	14 (53.85)	27 (67.50)	10 (62.50)	19 (50.00)
2.	No	24 (38.71)	24 (44.44)	11 (22.45)	12 (32.43)	21 (56.76)	20 (48.78)	8 (32.00)	11 (44.00)	12 (46.15)	13 (32.50)	6 (37.50)	19 (50.00)
3.	Total	62 (100.00)	54 (100.00)	49 (100.00)	37 (100.00)	37 (100.00)	41 (100.00)	25 (100.00)	25 (100.00)	26 (100.00)	40 (100.00)	16 (100.00)	38 (100.00)

Source: Compiled from the data collected from field work.

'B' people are more in Telangana and whereas in Andhra region category 'B' and 'D' are more in the activities of PRIs.

Table 6.2 discusses the caste-wise and region-wise distribution of opinion towards attending the grama sabha. The table reveals that Rayalaseema the majority of the respondents 38 and 30 belonging to category 'A' and 'B' are participating in the meetings of grama sabha. It is also identified that the majority 28 respondents belonging to category 'C' are not attending the meetings of gram sabha.

In Telangana region, majority of the respondents, 21 belonging to category 'B' and 17 respondents belonging to category 'D' are attending the meetings of gram sabha. The table also reveals that the lowest number of 8 and 11 respondents belonging to category 'C' and 'D' are not attending the meetings of grama sabha.

In Andhra region, the majority of respondents i.e., 27 belonging to category 'B' and 18 belonging to category 'D' are attending the meetings of grama sabha. 46.15% of respondents belonging to category 'A' and 32.50% of respondents belonging to category 'B' are not attending the meetings of grama sabha.

The over all findings of the table is that in Rayalaseema majority of people belonging to category 'A' and 'B' are attending the meeting of grama sabha. It is important to these that the majority of the rural development programmes is to be channalised and prepared through grama sabha. In Telangana and Andhra regions people belonging to category 'B' and 'D' are attending the meetings of grama sabha and participating in the development of grama panchayats.

Table 6.3 discusses the opinion-wise distribution of respondents regarding to reasons for not attending meetings of grama sabhas. Reasons for not attending are faction, ignorance, casteism, ignorance and politics.[4] In Rayalaseema from category 'A', 37.10% of respondents are not attending the meetings of

Table 6.3: Opinion-wise Distribution of Respondents Regarding to Reasons for not Attending Meetings of Grama Sabhas

		Rayala Seema Backward Caste				Telangana Backward Caste				Andhra Backward Caste			
		A	B	C	D	A	B	C	D	A	B	C	D
S. No	Opinion	Frequency	Frequ-ency	Frequ-ency	Frequ-ency	Frequ-ency	Frequ-ency	Frequ-ency	Frequ-ency	Frequ-ency	Frequ-ency	Frequ-ency	Frequ-ency
1.	Faction	21 (33.87)	13 (24.07)	12 (24.49)	9 (24.32)	13 (35.14)	15 (36.59)	10 (40.00)	6 (24.00)	6 (23.08)	20 (50.00)	6 (37.50)	10 (26.32)
2.	Casteism	23 (37.10)	16 (29.63)	19 (38.78)	12 (32.43)	15 (40.54)	18 (43.90)	7 (28.00)	7 (28.00)	7 (26.92)	7 (17.50)	4 (25.00)	9 (23.68)
3.	Ignorance	12 (19.35)	18 (33.33)	15 (30.61)	4 (10.81)	7 (18.92)	6 (14.63)	3 (12.00)	5 (20.00)	6 (23.08)	3 (7.50)	3 (18.75)	11 (28.95)
4.	Politics	6 (9.68)	7 (12.96)	3 (6.12)	12 (32.43)	2 (5.41)	2 (4.88)	5 (20.00)	7 (28.00)	7 (26.92)	10 (25.00)	3 (18.75)	8 (21.05)
5.	Total	62 (100.00)	54 (100.00)	49 (100.00)	37 (100.00)	37 (100.00)	41 (100.00)	25 (100.00)	25 (100.00)	26 (100.00)	40 (100.00)	16 (100.00)	38 (100.00)

Source: Compiled from the data collected from field work.

grama sabhas due to casteism followed by 33.87% due to faction, 19.35% due to ignorance and only 9.68% due to politics. It is identified from the table that 33.33% of respondents belonging to category 'B' are not attending grama sabhas due to ignorance. Nearly 38.78% respondents belonging to category 'C' are of the opinion that they are not attending due to casteism. Respondents belonging to category 'D' are not attending due to casteism and politics.

In Telangana the respondents in more number belonging to category 'A', 'B' and 'C' are not attending due to casteism, where as respondents belonging to category 'C' are not attending due to faction. So far as consist of Andhra region, the respondents belonging to category 'A' i.e., 26.72% are not attending due to politics. Respondents belonging to category 'B' and 'C' in more number i.e., 90% and 37.50% are not attending due to faction respectively. The highest number of respondents 11 belonging to category 'D' are not attending the meetings of grama sabha due to ignorance.

The over all observation of the table is that casteism and politics are the obstacles in the working of grama sabhas. It is also identified that the most backward castes are affected by casteism and faction and whereas the higher castes within OBCs are not participating due to politics and particularly by the involvement of lower castes. The lower castes are able to participate in PRIs only by the provisions of reservation to OBCs.

Table 6.4 discusses the distribution of opinion of respondents towards whether questions asked or not asked in the meetings of grama sabhas. In Rayalaseema respondents belonging to category 'A', 35.48% are not asking any questions in grama sabhas. 40.74% of respondents belonging to category 'B', 24.49% belonging to category 'C' and only 18.92% belonging to category 'D' are not asking any questions.

In Telangana region, 48.65% of respondents belonging to category 'A', 51.22% belonging to category 'B', 24% belonging to category 'C' and 32% belonging to category 'D' are not asking any questions in grama sabhas.

In Andhra region 10 respondents belonging to category 'A', 8 respondents belonging to category 'B', 7 belonging to category 'C' and 14 belonging to category 'D' are not asking any questions in the meetings of grama sabhas.

The over all observation of the table is that more number of respondents belonging to category 'A' and 'B' and less number of respondents belonging to category 'C' and 'D' are asking questions in the meetings of grama sabhas.

Table 6.5 discusses the distributions of respondent's awareness towards the powers of panchayat raj institutions in the study area. The table reveals that in Rayalaseema, respondents belonging to category 'A' with 75.81% are not aware of powers of panchayat raj institutions, followed by 37.04% of respondents belonging to category 'B'. Whereas the more number of respondents i.e., 81.63% and 78.38% belonging to category 'C' and 'D' respectively are aware of powers of panchayat raj institutions.

In Telangana region the highest number of respondents i.e. 54.05% belonging to category 'A', are not aware of the power of panchayat raj institutions. Whereas the highest number of respondents i.e., 53.66%, 80.00%, 64.00% belonging to category 'B', 'C' and 'D' respectively are aware of powers of panchayat raj institutions.

In Andhra region, the highest number 61.54% of respondents belonging to category 'A' are not aware of powers of panchayat raj institutions. Whereas the highest number i.e., 75%, 62.50% and 60.53% belonging to category 'B', 'C' and 'D' are aware of the power of panchayat raj institutions.

Table 6.4: Distribution of Opinion of Respondents towards whether Questions Asked or not Asked in the Meetings of Grama Sabhas

		Rayala Seema Backward Caste				Telangana Backward Caste				Andhra Backward Caste			
		A	B	C	D	A	B	C	D	A	B	C	D
S.No	Opinion	Frequency	Frequ-ency	Frequ-ency	Frequ-ency	Frequ-ency	Frequ-ency	Frequ-ency	Frequ-ency	Frequ-ency	Frequ-ency	Frequ-ency	Frequ-ency
1.	Yes	40 (64.52)	32 (59.26)	37 (75.51)	30 (81.08)	19 (51.35)	20 (48.78)	19 (76.00)	17 (68.00)	16 (61.54)	32 (80.00)	9 (56.25)	24 (63.16)
2.	No	22 (35.48)	22 (40.74)	12 (24.49)	7 (18.92)	18 (48.65)	21 (51.22)	6 (24.00)	8 (32.00)	10 (38.46)	8 (20.00)	7 (43.75)	14 (36.84)
3.	Total	62 (100.00)	54 (100.00)	49 (100.00)	37 (100.00)	37 (100.00)	41 (100.00)	25 (100.00)	25 (100.00)	26 (100.00)	40 (100.00)	16 (100.00)	38 (100.00)

Source: Compiled from the data collected from field work.

Table 6.5: Distributions of Respondent's Awareness towards the Powers of Panchayat Raj Institutions in the Study Area

		Rayala Seema Backward Caste				Telangana Backward Caste				Andhra Backward Caste			
		A	B	C	D	A	B	C	D	A	B	C	D
S.No	Opinion	Frequency	Frequ-ency	Frequ-ency	Frequ-ency	Frequ-ency	Frequ-ency	Frequ-ency	Frequ-ency	Frequ-ency	Frequ-ency	Frequ-ency	Frequ-ency
1.	Yes	15 (24.19)	34 (62.96)	40 (81.63)	29 (78.38)	17 (45.95)	22 (53.66)	20 (80.00)	16 (64.00)	10 (38.46)	30 (75.00)	10 (62.50)	23 (60.53)
2.	No	47 (75.81)	20 (37.04)	9 (18.37)	8 (21.62)	20 (54.05)	19 (46.34)	5 (20.00)	9 (36.00)	16 (61.54)	10 (25.00)	6 (37.50)	15 (39.47)
3.	Total	62 (100.00)	54 (100.00)	49 (100.00)	37 (100.00)	37 (100.00)	41 (100.00)	25 (100.00)	25 (100.00)	26 (100.00)	40 (100.00)	16 (100.00)	38 (100.00)

Source: Compiled from the data collected from field work.

The over all observations of the table is that the majority of the respondents belonging to category 'A' in all the three regions are not aware of powers of PRI's and the highest number of respondents belonging to category 'B', 'C' and 'D' in all the three religions are aware of power of panchayat raj institutions.

Table 6.6 discusses the opinion towards official's cooperation in the working of panchayat raj institutions. The table reveals that in Rayalaseema the lowest number, 10 respondents with 16.13% belonging to category 'A' are able to get the co-operation from officers. On the other hand 52 respondents with 83.87% are not getting cooperation's from the officers. It is also identified from the table that the majority of the respondents belonging to category 'B', 'C' and 'D' are getting cooperation from the officials.

In Telangana, respondents belonging to category 'A' in highest number are not getting cooperation from the official on the other hand the respondents belonging to category 'C' and 'D' are in more number getting cooperation from the officials concerned.

In Andhra region the respondents belonging to category 'B' and 'D' are getting cooperation from the official. On the other hand respondents belonging to category 'B' in more number are not getting cooperation from the officials.

The over all observations of the table is that in all the three regions, the highest number of respondents belonging to category 'A' are not in a position of getting cooperation from the official working in the institutions of panchayat raj. It is also found that the majority of respondents belonging to category 'B', 'C' and 'D' in all the regions are getting cooperation from the officials in the institutions of panchayat raj.

Table 6.7 discusses the opinion towards exercising franchise. The table reveals that in Rayalaseema, the majority of respondents from all categories are exercising franchise in

Table 6.6: Opinion towards Official's Co-operation in the Working of Panchayat Raj Institutions

		Rayala Seema Backward Caste				Telangana Backward Caste				Andhra Backward Caste			
		A	B	C	D	A	B	C	D	A	B	C	D
Sl. No	Opinion	Frequency	Frequency	Frequency	Frequency	Frequency	Frequency	Frequency	Frequency	Frequency	Frequency	Frequency	Frequency
1.	Yes	10 (16.13)	31 (57.41)	38 (77.55)	28 (75.68)	15 (40.54)	21 (51.22)	18 (72.00)	14 (56.00)	12 (46.15)	28 (70.00)	8 (50.00)	21 (55.26)
2.	No	52 (83.87)	23 (42.59)	11 (22.45)	9 (24.32)	22 (59.46)	20 (48.78)	7 (28.00)	11 (44.00)	14 (53.85)	12 (30.00)	8 (50.00)	17 (44.74)
3.	Total	62 (100.00)	54 (100.00)	49 (100.00)	37 (100.00)	37 (100.00)	41 (100.00)	25 (100.00)	25 (100.00)	26 (100.00)	40 (100.00)	16 (100.00)	38 (100.00)

Source: Compiled from the data collected from field work.

Table 6.7: Opinion towards Exercising Franchise

		Rayala Seema Backward Caste				Telangana Backward Caste				Andhra Backward Caste			
		A	B	C	D	A	B	C	D	A	B	C	D
Sl. No.	Opinion	Frequency	Frequency	Frequency	Frequency	Frequency	Frequency	Frequency	Frequency	Frequency	Frequency	Frequency	Frequency
1.	Yes	48 (77.42)	28 (51.85)	32 (65.31)	30 (81.08)	30 (81.08)	24 (58.54)	20 (80.00)	18 (72.00)	21 (80.77)	30 (75.00)	12 (75.00)	32 (84.21)
2.	No	14 (22.58)	26 (48.15)	17 (34.69)	7 (18.92)	7 (18.92)	17 (41.46)	5 (20.00)	7 (28.00)	5 (19.23)	10 (25.00)	4 (25.00)	6 (15.79)
3.	Total	62 (100.00)	54 (100.00)	49 (100.00)	37 (100.00)	3 (100.00)	41 (100.00)	25 (100.00)	25 (100.00)	26 (100.00)	40 (100.00)	16 (100.00)	38 (100.00)

Source: Compiled from the data collected from field work.

different types of education i.e., 77.42% belonging to the category 'A', 51.85% belonging to category 'B', 65.31% belonging to category 'C' and 81.08% belonging to category 'A'.

In Telangana, the majority of respondents from all the categories are exercising their franchise in different types of education including panchayat raj i.e., 81.08% belonging to category 'A', 58.54% belonging to category 'B', 80.00% belonging to category 'C' and 72.00% belonging to category 'D'.

In Andhra region on par with the other two regions, the majority of respondents from all the categories are exercising their franchise.

The over all observations of the table is that the respondents belonging to backward categories in majority are exercising their franchise and there exists the political participation and process of backward castes.

Table 6.8 discusses the contest of election-wise distribution of opinion. It is identified from the table that in Rayalaseema the majority of respondents in highest number are not sting the elections in the institutions of panchayat raj.

In Telangana, the majority of respondents from all the categories is highest number are contesting in different types of elections.

In Andhra region, the highest number of respondents from all the categories are cultivating the different types of elections.

The over all observations of the table is that the majority of the respondents belonging to category 'A' are not contesting the election in the institutions of panchayat raj. Whereas in Telangana and Andhra region the highest number of respondents belonging to backward castes are contesting the elections.

Table 6.9 discusses that the canvas in the election-wise distribution of opinion in the study area. In Rayalaseema the

Table 6.8: Contest of Election-wise Distribution of Opinion

		Rayala Seema Backward Caste				Telangana Backward Caste				Andhra Backward Caste			
		A	B	C	D	A	B	C	D	A	B	C	D
Sl No	Opinion	Frequency	Frequency	Frequency	Frequency	Frequency	Frequency	Frequency	Frequency	Frequency	Frequency	Frequency	Frequency
1.	Yes	20 (32.26)	20 (37.04)	19 (38.78)	15 (40.54)	19 (51.35)	23 (56.10)	19 (76.00)	18 (72.00)	18 (69.23)	30 (75.00)	14 (87.50)	31 (81.58)
2.	No	42 (67.74)	34 (62.96)	30 (61.22)	22 (59.46)	18 (48.65)	18 (43.90)	6 (24.00)	7 (28.00)	8 (30.77)	10 (25.00)	2 (12.50)	7 (18.4
3.	Total	62 (100.00)	54 (100.00)	49 (100.00)	37 (100.00)	37 (100.00)	41 (100.00)	25 (100.00)	25 (100.00)	26 (100.00)	40 (100.00)	16 (100.00)	38 (100.00)

Source: Compiled from the data collected from field work.

Table 6.9: Canvas in the Election-wise Distribution of Opinion in the Study Area

		Rayala Seema Backward Caste				Telangana Backward Caste				Andhra Backward Caste			
		A	B	C	D	A	B	C	D	A	B	C	D
Sl. No.	Opinion	Frequency	Frequency	Frequency	Frequency	Frequency	Frequency	Frequency	Frequency	Frequency	Frequency	Frequency	Frequency
1.	Yes	28 (45.16)	18 (33.33)	17 (34.69)	30 (81.08)	18 (48.65)	24 (58.54)	21 (84.00)	17 (68.00)	16 (61.54)	25 (62.50)	8 (50.00)	19 (50.00)
2.	No	34 (54.84)	36 (66.67)	32 (65.31)	7 (18.92)	19 (51.35)	17 (41.46)	4 (16.00)	8 (32.00)	10 (38.46)	15 (37.50)	8 (50.00)	19 (50.00)
3.	Total	62 (100.00)	54 (100.00)	49 (100.00)	37 (100.00)	37 (100.00)	41 (100.00)	25 (100.00)	25 (100.00)	26 (100.00)	40 (100.00)	16 (100.00)	38 (100.00)

Source: Compiled from the data collected from field work.

majority of the respondents belonging to category 'A' with 54.84%, category 'B' with 66.67% and category 'C' with 65.31% are not canvassing in any type of elections. It is found that only respondents belonging to category 'D' are canvassing in the elections.

In Telangana, respondents belonging to category 'A' with 51.35% are not canvassing in the elections. On the other hand respondents belonging to category 'B' with 58.54%, category 'C' with 84.00% and 68.00% belonging to category 'A' are canvassing in the different types of elections.

In Andhra region, the highest number of respondents from all the category belonging to backward castes are canvassing in the different types of elections.

The findings of the table are that in Rayalaseema the majority of backward castes are not actively participating in the electoral process. Whereas, in Telangana, except category 'A', other backward castes are actively participating in the elections and in Andhra region the majority backward castes are actively participating in the elections.

Table 6.10 discusses the opinion towards the mobilisation of money-wise distribution of respondents. It is observed from the table that in Rayalaseema the majority of respondents from all the categories are not mobilising money during the elections i.e., 43 respondents belonging to category 'A', 23 belonging to category 'B', 28 belonging to category 'C' and 21 belonging to category 'D'.

In Telangana, the table reveals that the majority of backward castes are mobilising money during the elections, which means the backward castes in Telangana are activity participating in the political process i.e., 20 respondents belonging to category 'A', 22 belonging to category 'B', 19 belonging to category 'C' and 18 belonging to category 'D'.

In Andhra region, it is observed from the table that only 38.46% of respondents belonging to category 'A' are mobilising money during elections. Respondents belonging to category 'B' only 50% are mobilising and from categories 'C' and 'D' the majority of respondents are mobilising money during elections.

The finding of the table is that the majority of respondents belonging to backward castes in Rayalaseema and Andhra region belonging to category 'A' are not mobilising money during elections. In Telangana the majority of respondents are mobilising money during elections. In Andhra region respondents belonging to category 'B', 'C' and 'D' are mobilizing money during elections. In Rayalaseema the backward castes political participation is controlled by the dominant Reddy and Kamma castes.

Table 6.11 discusses the opinion towards political affiliation-wise distribution of respondents. It is observed from the table that in Rayalaseema, the highest number of respondents 58.06% belonging to category 'A' do not have political affiliation to any political party. On the other hand the majority of respondents from other backward castes have political affiliation to different political parties.

In Telangana, the highest number of respondents 51.22% belonging to category 'B' do not have political affiliations to any political party. On the other hand the majority of respondents belonging to category 'A', 'C' and 'D' have political affiliations. In Andhra region, it is observed from the table that the majority of respondents 52.63% belonging to category 'D' do not have political affiliations. On the other hand the majority of respondents belonging to category 'A', 'B' and 'C' have political affiliations to different political parties.

The finding of the table is that respondents belonging to category 'A' in I Rayalaseema, category 'B' in Telangana and category 'D' in Andhra region are not having any political affiliation to any political parties. On the other hand respondents

Table 6.10: Opinion towards the Mobilisation of Money-wise Distribution of Respondents

		Rayala Seema Backward Caste				Telangana Backward Caste				Andhra Backward Caste			
		A	B	C	D	A	B	C	D	A	B	C	D
Sl. No.	Opinion	Frequ ency	Frequ-ency	Frequ-ency	Frequ-ency	Frequ-ency	Frequ-ency	Frequ-ency	Frequ-ency	Frequ-ency	Frequ-ency	Frequ-ency	Frequ-ency
1.	Yes	19 (30.65)	21 (38.89)	20 (40.82)	16 (43.24)	20 (54.05)	22 (53.66)	19 (76.00)	18 (72.00)	10 (38.46)	20 (50.00)	10 (62.50)	25 (65.79)
2.	No	43 (69.35)	23 (42.59)	29 (59.18)	21 (56.76)	17 (45.95)	19 (46.34)	6 (24.00)	7 (28.00)	16 (61.54)	20 (50.00)	6 (37.50)	13 (34.21)
3.	Total	62 (100.00)	54 (100.00)	49 (100.00)	37 (100.00)	37 (100.00)	41 (100.00)	25 (100.000	25 (100.00)	26 (100.00)	40 (100.00)	16 (100.00)	38 (100.00)

Source: Compiled from the data collected from field work.

Table 6.11: Opinion towards Political Affiliation-wise Distribution of Respondents

		Rayala Seema Backward Caste				Telangana Backward Caste				Andhra Backward Caste			
		A	B	C	D	A	B	C	D	A	B	C	D
Sl. No.	Opinion	Frequ ency	Frequ-ency	Frequ-ency	Frequ-ency	Frequ-ency	Frequ-ency	Frequ-ency	Frequ-ency	Frequ-ency	Frequ-ency	Frequ-ency	Frequ-ency
1.	Yes	26 (41.94)	29 (53.70)	30 (61.22)	25 (67.57)	27 (72.97)	20 (48.78)	18 (72.00)	19 (76.00)	20 (76.92)	25 (62.50)	10 (62.50)	18 (47.37)
2.	No	36 (58.06)	25 (46.30)	19 (38.78)	12 (32.43)	10 (27.03)	21 (51.22)	7 (28.00)	9 (36.00)	6 (23.08)	15 (37.50)	6 (37.50)	20 (52.63)
3.	Total	62 (100.00)	54 (100.00)	49 (100.00)	37 (100.00)	37 (100.00)	41 (100.00)	25 (100.00)	25 (100.00)	26 (100.00)	40 (100.00)	16 (100.00)	38 (100.00)

ource: Compiled from the data collected from field work.

belonging to category 'B', 'C' and 'D' in Rayalaseema , category 'A', 'C' and 'D' in Telangana and category 'A', 'B' and 'C' in Andhra region have political affiliation in different political parties. To understand the level of political participation and political process of the people can be understood and determine based on the level of political affiliation of the people.

Table 6.12 discusses the opinion towards why dominant among BCs elected-wise distribute of respondents in the study area.

It is observed from the table that in Rayalaseema. The category 'A' respondents in majority are of the opinion that due to mobilisation and agricultural resources the dominant castes are being elected and other castes within BCs are neglected. The respondents belonging to category 'B' are of the opinion that due to agricultural resources and higher social status. The dominant castes are being elected. The respondents belonging to category 'C' and 'D' are of the opinion that due to agriculture resources and higher social status the dominant caste people are being elected.

In Telangana, it is observed from the table that the majority of respondents from all the category belonging to backwards expressed that due to agricultural resources and numerical strength the dominant castes people are being elected to different types of election.

In Andhra region, the majority of the respondents are of the opinion that due to agricultural resources and numerical strength of the caste, the dominant castes among OBCs are being elected.

The findings of the table are that agricultural resources and numerical strength of the castes and also the social status of the caste within BCs are the important factors to occupy the position in the institutions of panchayat raj.

Table 6.13 discusses opinion towards the unity among upper caste-wise distribution of respondents. It is observed from the the

Table 6.12: Opinion towards why Dominant among BCs Elected-wise Distribute of Respondents in the Study Area

		Rayala Seema Backward Caste				Telangana Backward Caste				Andhra Backward Caste			
		A	B	C	D	A	B	C	D	A	B	C	D
Sl. No.	Opinion	Frequ ency	Frequ-ency	Frequ-ency	Frequ-ency	Frequ-ency	Frequ-ency	Frequ-ency	Frequ-ency	Frequ-ency	Frequ-ency	Frequ-ency	Frequ-ency
1.	Agricultural Resources	20 (32.26)	15 (27.78)	11 (22.45)	10 (27.03)	11 (29.73)	10 (24.39)	10 (40.00)	5 (20.00)	8 (30.77)	18 (45.00)	7 (43.75)	12 (31.58)
2.	More Number of Caste	21 (33.87)	14 (25.93)	20 (40.82)	11 (29.73)	17 (45.95)	18 (43.90)	6 (24.00)	8 (32.00)	5 (19.23)	9 (22.50)	3 (18.75)	7 (18.42)
3.	Higher Social Status	11 (17.74)	15 (27.78)	15 (30.61)	5 (13.51)	5 (13.51)	5 (12.20)	4 (16.00)	6 (24.00)	5 (19.23)	5 (12.50)	3 (18.75)	10 (26.32)
4.	Part Support	10 (16.13)	10 (18.52)	3 (6.12)	11 (29.73)	4 (10.81)	8 (19.51)	5 (20.00)	6 (24.00)	8 (30.77)	8 (20.00)	3 (18.75)	9 (23.68)
5.	Total	62 (100.00)	54 (100.00)	49 (100.00)	37 (100.00)	37 (100.00)	41 (100.00)	25 (100.00)	25 (100.00)	26 (100.00)	40 (100.00)	16 (100.00)	38 (100.00)

Source: Compiled from the data collected from field work.

Table 6.13: Opinion towards the Unity among Upper Caste-wise Distribution of Respondents

		Rayala Seema Backward Caste				Telangana Backward Caste				Andhra Backward Caste			
		A	B	C	D	A	B	C	D	A	B	C	D
Sl. No.	Opinion	Frequ ency	Frequ-ency	Frequ-ency	Frequ-ency	Frequ-ency	Frequ-ency	Frequ-ency	Frequ-ency	Frequ-ency	Frequ-ency	Frequ-ency	Frequ-ency
1.	Yes	39 (62.90)	30 (55.56)	14 (28.57)	31 (83.78)	19 (51.35)	21 (51.22)	6 (24.00)	8 (32.00)	15 (57.69)	31 (77.50)	9 (56.25)	22 (57.89)
2.	No	23 (37.10)	24 (44.44)	35 (71.43)	6 (16.22)	18 (48.65)	20 (48.78)	19 (76.00)	17 (68.00)	11 (42.31)	9 (22.50)	7 (43.75)	16 (42.11)
3.	Total	62 (100.00)	54 (100.00)	49 (100.00)	37 (100.00)	37 (100.00)	41 (100.00)	25 (100.00)	25 (100.00)	26 (100.00)	40 (100.00)	16 (100.00)	38 (100.00)

Source: Compiled from the data collected from field work.

table that in Rayalaseema the highest number of respondents belonging to category 'A', 'B' and 'D' expressed that there is high unity among the upper castes. As a result they are able to maintain dominance in the villages and capturing the political power.

In Telangana, receipt respondents belonging to category 'C' all other categories is the highest number agreed that there is an higher level of unity and understanding among the upper castes.

In Andhra region, the highest number of respondents from all categories are of the opinion that there is unity and lives level of understanding among the upper castes. Therefore, the upper castes still maintaining the dominance in the working of panchayat raj institutions.

The over all observations of the table is that in Rayalaseema and Telengana the people belonging to category 'C' are feeling that they are also belonging to upper castes and they do not have backward feeling. It is also observed from the table that in the study area, the upper castes belonging to category 'A', 'B' and 'D' feels that there is no unity among the backward castes and as a result they are not able to capture the political power in the institutions of panchayat raj institutions.

Table 6.14 discusses the opinion towards reasons for the non-involvement of weaker sections in PRI's-wise distribution of respondents. In Rayalaseema majority of respondents from all the categories are not able to involve in the institutions of PRIs due to illiteracy and low economic conditions.

In Telangana, the majority of the respondents are also not entering in the working of PRIs due to illiteracy, and low economic conditions.

In Andhra region illiteracy and low economic conditions and dominant of upper castes are the factors, which are preventing the weaker sections in capturing the political power.

Table 614: Opinion towards Reasons for the Non-Involvement of Weaker Sections in PRI's-wise Distribution of Respondents

		Rayala Seema Backward Caste				Telangana Backward Caste				Andhra Backward Caste			
		A	B	C	D	A	B	C	D	A	B	C	D
Sl. No.	Opinion	Frequency	Frequency	Frequency	Frequency	Frequency	Frequency	Frequency	Frequency	Frequency	Frequency	Frequency	Frequency
1.	Illiteracy	20 (32.26)	10 (18.52)	10 (20.41)	9 (24.32)	10 (27.03)	11 (26.83)	11 (44.00)	8 (32.00)	8 (30.77)	17 (42.50)	7 (43.75)	10 (26.32)
2.	Economy	20 (32.26)	19 (35.19)	19 (38.78)	12 (32.43)	16 (43.24)	17 (41.46)	5 (20.00)	5 (20.00)	6 (23.08)	10 (25.00)	3 (18.75)	9 (23.68)
3.	Dominance of Upper Castes	11 (17.74)	13 (24.07)	17 (34.69)	6 (16.22)	7 (18.92)	7 (17.07)	4 (16.00)	5 (20.00)	4 (15.38)	6 (15.00)	2 (12.50)	9 (23.68)
4.	Conspiracy of Upper Castes	10 (16.13)	12 (22.22)	3 (6.12)	10 (27.12)	4 (10.81)	7 (17.07)	5 (20.00)	7 (28.00)	8 (30.77)	7 (17.50)	4 (25.00)	10 (26.32)
5.	Total	61 (100.00)	54 (100.00)	49 (100.00)	37 (100.00)	37 (100.00)	41 (100.00)	25 (100.00)	25 (100.00)	26 (100.00)	40 (100.00)	16 (100.00)	38 (100.00

Source: Compiled from the data collected from field work.

The findings of the table are that the weaker sections are not able to capture the political power due to illiteracy, low income and the dominance of upper castes.

Table 6.15 discusses the opinion towards reservation to OBCs is helped for the welfare of BCC's-wise distributions of respondents. In Rayalaseema, the category 'A' respondents expressed that the reservation provisions in PRIs have not achieved its goals. On the other hand the upper castes within BC's such as category 'B', 'C' and 'D' are of the opinion that the reservation provision are caused in achieving the welfare of their categories.

In Telangana, the respondents belonging to category 'A' have negative opinion towards the reservation provisions in PRIs and the other categories have positive opinion.

In Andhra region, the respondents belonging to category 'A' have negative opinion and other categories have positive opinion.

The over all observation of the table is that in Rayalaseema, Telangana and Andhra region the reservation provision are not able to achieve the welfare of category 'A' and on the other hand able to achieve the welfare of category 'B', 'C' and 'D' people.

Table 6.16 discusses the opinion towards involvement in PRIs led for crime-wise distribution of respondents. It is observed that in Rayalaseema majority of the respondents from all the categories are of the opinion that the involvement in the working of PRIs led by criminal charges i.e., respondents belonging to category 'A' is 61.29%, 55.50% belonging to category 'B', 69.39% belonging to category 'C' and 83.78% belonging to category 'D'.

In Telangana, the majority of respondents are of the view that their involvement in the working of PRIs led for the criminal charges by opponents.

Table 6.15: Opinion towards reservation to OBCs is Helped for the Welfare of BCC's-wise Distributions of Respondents

		Rayala Seema Backward Caste				Telangana Backward Caste				Andhra Backward Caste			
		A	B	C	D	A	B	C	D	A	B	C	D
Sl. No.	Opinion	Frequency	Frequency	Frequency	Frequency	Frequency	Frequency	Frequency	Frequency	Frequency	Frequency	Frequency	Frequency
1.	Yes	24 (38.71)	31 (57.41)	35 (71.43)	33 (89.19)	15 (40.54)	22 (53.66)	19 (76.00)	17 (68.00)	10 (38.46)	31 (77.5)	10 (62.50)	31 (81.58)
2.	No	38 (61.29)	23 (42.59)	14 (28.57)	4 (10.81)	22 (59.46)	19 (46.34)	6 (24.00)	8 (32.00)	16 (61.54)	9 (22.5)	6 (37.50)	7 (18.42)
3.	Total	62 (100.00)	54 (100.00)	49 (100.00)	37 (100.00)	37 (100.00)	41 (100.00)	25 (100.00)	25 (100.00)	26 (100.00)	40 (100.00)	16 (100.00)	38 (100.00)

Source: Compiled from the data collected from field work.

Table 6.16: Opinion towards Involvement in PRIs led for Crime-wise Distribution of Respondents

		Rayala Seema Backward Caste				Telangana Backward Caste				Andhra Backward Caste			
		A	B	C	D	A	B	C	D	A	B	C	D
Sl. No.	Opinion	Frequency	Frequency	Frequency	Frequency	Frequency	Frequency	Frequency	Frequency	Frequency	Frequency	Frequency	Frequency
1.	Yes	24 (38.71)	31 (57.41)	35 (71.43)	33 (89.19)	15 (40.54)	22 (53.66)	19 (76.00)	17 (68.00)	10 (38.46)	31 (77.5)	10 (62.50)	31 (81.58)
2.	No	38 (61.29)	23 (42.59)	14 (28.57)	4 (10.81)	22 (59.46)	19 (46.34)	6 (24.00)	8 (32.00)	16 (61.54)	9 (22.5)	6 (37.50)	7 (18.42)
3.	Total	62 (100.00)	54 (100.00)	49 (100.00)	37 (100.00)	37 (100.00)	41 (100.00)	25 (100.00)	25 (100.00)	26 (100.00)	40 (100.00)	16 (100.00)	38 (100.00)

Source: Compiled from the data collected from field work.

In Andhra region, the respondents belonging to category 'C' are not facing any criminal charges by involving in the working of PRIs. And other category respondents i.e., 61.54% belonging to category 'A', 75.00% belonging to category 'B' and 63.16% belonging to category 'D' are facing the criminal charges.

It is the important finding of the study that in all the regions the majority of respondents belonging to most backward categories are facing the criminal charges. The policy-makers have to think this aspect very seriously.

Table 6.17 discusses the opinion towards whether PRIs caused for the domination of upper castes. It is identified from the table that in Rayalaseema. The highest number of respondents from all the categories expressed that the present system of panchayat raj institutions caused for the domination of upper castes i.e., 66.13% of respondents belonging to category 'A', 62.96% belonging to category 'B', 71.43% belonging to category 'C' and 54.05% belonging to category 'D'.

In Telangana the majority of respondents from all the categories expressed that the present system of panchayat raj has facilitated or the dominance of upper castes.

In Andhra region, the majority of respondents expressed that the introduction of panchayat raj system further depend the dominance of upper castes over the weaker sections.

The finding of the table is that in all the three regions (study area). The present system of panchayat raj system has caused for the dominance of upper castes over the lower backward castes.

Table 6.18 discusses the opinion towards to whom the forward castes support-wise distribution of respondents. It is observed from the table that in Rayalaseema, the majority of respondents expressed that the forward castes are supporting the category 'C' and category 'D' people, who happens to be the upper castes within backwards.

Table 6.17: Opinion towards whether PRIs Caused for the Domination of Upper Caste

		Rayala Seema Backward Caste				Telangana Backward Caste				Andhra Backward Caste			
		A	B	C	D	A	B	C	D	A	B	C	D
Sl. No	Opinion	Frequency	Frequency	Frequency	Frequency	Frequency	Frequency	Frequency	Frequency	Frequency	Frequency	Frequency	Frequency
1.	Yes	41 (66.13)	34 (62.96)	35 (71.43)	20 (54.05)	28 (75.68)	25 (60.98)	22 (88.00)	21 (84.00)	21 (80.77)	31 (77.50)	10 (62.50)	30 (78.95)
2.	No	21 (33.87)	20 (37.04)	14 (28.57)	17 (45.95)	9 (24.32)	16 (39.02)	3 (12.00)	4 (16.00)	5 (19.23)	9 (22.50)	6 (37.50)	8 (21.05)
3.	Total	62 (100.00)	54 (100.000	49 (100.00)	37 (100.00)	37 (100.00)	41 (100.00)	25 (100.00)	25 (100.00)	26 (100.00)	40 (100.00)	16 (100.00)	38 (100.00)

Source: Compiled from the data collected from field work.

Table 6.18: Opinion towards to whom the Forward Castes Support-wise Distribution of Respondents

Sl. No.		Rayala Seema Backward Caste				Telangana Backward Caste				Andhra Backward Caste			
		A	B	C	D	A	B	C	D	A	B	C	D
1.	Cat-A	10 (16.13)	10 (18.52)	3 (6.12)	10 (27.03)	4 (10.81)	7 (17.07)	5 (20.00)	7 (28.00)	6 (23.08)	7 (17.50)	4 (25.00)	10 (26.32)
2.	Cat-B	11 (17.74)	13 (24.07)	17 (34.69)	6 (16.22)	7 (18.92)	7 (17.07)	4 (16.00)	5 (20.00)	4 (15.38)	6 (15.00)	2 (12.50)	9 (23.68)
3.	Cat-D	20 (32.26)	19 (35.19)	19 (38.78)	12 (32.43)	16 (43.24)	17 (41.46)	5 (20.00)	5 (20.00)	8 (30.77)	10 (25.00)	3 (18.75)	9 (23.68)
4.	Total	62 (100.00)	54 (100.00)	49 (100.00)	37 (100.00)	37 (100.00)	41 (100.00)	25 (100.00)	25 (100.00)	26 (100.00)	40 (100.00)	16 (100.00)	38 (100.00)

Source: Compiled from the data collected from field work.

In Telangana, the majority of respondents from all the categories are of the opinion that the forward extend their support only to the castes who have higher social status within backward castes i.e., category 'C' and 'D'.

In Andhra region, the majority of the respondents are of the opinion that the forward castes are supporting the castes with higher social status within BCs.

The over all observation of the table is that in the study areas, the upper caste people are supporting the people with higher social status within backward castes. It is the important findings of the study. The lower castes are not getting support from the forward castes and as a result the upper castes within backwards are getting political positions.

Table 6.19 discusses the opinion towards whether rich in BC's capture the PRIs-wise distribution of respondents. The table reveals that in Rayalaseema, the majority of respondents from all the categories are of the opinion that the castes within backwards with high economic resources are capturing the positions in the institutions of panchayat raj institutions.

In Telangana and Andhra region are par with Rayalaseema, the majority of respondents expressed that the different positions in panchayat raj are being captured by the rich people within backwards.

The findings of the table is that in the study area the positions such as, ward member, presidents, MPTC, ZPTC and chairpersons from taluk and zilla panchayats under reserved categories for backward castes are captured and controlled by the rich people within BCs. Though there is a reservation provisions for backward castes, economically poor people within backwards are not able to enter in the institutions of Panchayat raj institutions.

Table 6.20 discusses the opinion towards whether the representatives in panchayat raj institution are extending the

Table 6.19: Opinion towards whether Rich in BC's Capture the PRIs-wise Distribution of Respondents

		Rayala Seema Backward Caste				Telangana Backward Caste				Andhra Backward Caste			
		A	B	C	D	A	B	C	D	A	B	C	D
Sl. No.	Opinion	Frequ ency	Frequ-ency	Frequ-ency	Frequ-ency	Frequ-ency	Frequ-ency	Frequ-ency	Frequ-ency	Frequ-ency	Frequ-ency	Frequ-ency	Frequ-ency
1.	Yes	40 (64.52)	31 (57.41)	35 (71.43)	17 (45.95)	27 (72.97)	25 (60.98)	20 (80.00)	19 (76.00)	21 (80.77)	29 (72.50)	10 (62.50)	28 (73.68)
2.	No	22 (35.48)	23 (42.59)	14 (28.57)	20 (54.05)	10 (27.03)	16 (39.00)	5 (20.00)	5 (20.00)	5 (19.23)	11 (27.50)	6 (37.50)	10 (26.32)
3.	Total	62 (100.00)	54 (100.00)	49 (100.00)	37 (100.00)	37 (100.00)	41 (100.00)	25 (100.00)	25 (100.00)	26 (100.00)	40 (100.00)	16 (100.00)	38 (100.00)

Source: Compiled from the data collected from field work.

Table 6.20: Opinion towards whether the Representatives in Panchayat Raj Institution are extending the Benefits to their Castes

		Rayala Seema Backward Caste				Telangana Backward Caste				Andhra Backward Caste			
		A	B	C	D	A	B	C	D	A	B	C	D
Sl. No.	Opinion	Frequ ency	Frequ-ency	Frequ-ency	Frequ-ency	Frequ-ency	Frequ-ency	Frequ-Ency	Frequ-ency	Frequ-ency	Frequ-ency	Frequ-ency	Frequ-ency
1.	Yes	42 (67.74)	30 (55.56)	35 (71.43)	17 (45.95)	26 (70.27)	25 (60.98)	18 (72.00)	18 (72.00)	20 (76.92)	30 (75.00)	10 (62.50)	27 (71.05)
2.	No	20 (32.26)	24 (44.44)	15 (28.57)	20 (54.05)	11 (29.73)	16 (39.08)	7 (28.00)	7 (28.00)	6 (23.08)	10 (25.00)	6 (37.50)	11 (28.95)
3.	Total	62 (100.00)	54 (100.00)	49 (100.00)	37 (100.00)	37 (100.00)	41 (100.00)	25 (100.00)	25 (100.000	26 (100.00)	40 (100.00)	16 (100.00)	38 (100.00)

Source: Compiled from the data collected from field work.

benefits to their castes. It is reveals from the table that in all the three regions, Rayalaseema, Telangana and Andhra, the majority of respondents from all the categories are of the opinion that the representatives in the institutions of panchayat raj are extending the programmes and benefits under reserved category to the caste that they belong. It shows that at the grass root level the political participation and process has caste based. Thus, the caste has become the primary aspects in capturing the political positions.

The over all observation of the table is that in the study area, the representatives are being elected with the caste composition and as a result they are extending their support to their caste people while implementing various developmental programmes.

Table 6.21 discusses the opinion towards as your caste do not represent you are not benefited-wise distribution of respondents. The table reveals that except respondents belonging to category 'C' and the other categories in the study area are of the opinion that they are not getting benefits of panchayat raj institutions as their caste do not represent.

The over all observation of the table is that there exist the caste based political representatives in the working of panchayat raj institutions. The people will get benefits of panchayat raj institutions if there is a representatives belonging to their caste.

Table 6.22 discusses the opinion towards who are the most affected castes in your village-wise distribution of respondents. The table reveals that in the study area the most of the respondents are of the opinion that the castes such as category 'A' and category 'B' are the most disadvantaged people. On the other hand the people belonging to category 'C' and 'D' are the most benefited castes under the reservation provisions in the institutions of panchayat raj.

Table 6.21: Opinion towards as your Caste do not Represent you are not Benefited-wise Distribution of Respondents

		Rayala Seema Backward Caste				Telangana Backward Caste				Andhra Backward Caste			
		A	B	C	D	A	B	C	D	A	B	C	D
Sl. No.	Opinion	Frequ ency	Frequ-ency	Frequ-ency	Frequ-ency	Frequ-ency	Frequ-ency	Frequ-Ency	Frequ-ency	Frequ-ency	Frequ-ency	Frequ-ency	Frequ-ency
1.	Yes	48 (77.42)	27 (50.00)	24 (48.98)	15 (40.54)	20 (54.05)	25 (60.98)	15 (60.00)	16 (64.00)	22 (84.62)	32 (80.00)	12 (75.00)	26 (68.42)
2.	No	14 (22.58)	27 (50.00)	25 (51.02)	22 (59.46)	11 (29.73)	16 (39.02)	10 (40.00)	8 (32.00)	4 (15.38)	8 (20.00)	4 (25.00)	12 (31.58)
3.	Total	62 (100.00)	54 (100.00)	49 (100.00)	37 (100.00)	37 (100.00)	41 (100.00)	25 (100.00)	25 (100.00)	26 (100.00)	40 (100.00)	16 (100.00)	38 (100.00)

Source: Compiled from the data collected from field work.

Table 6.22: Opinion towards who are the most Affected Castes in your Village-wise Distribution of Respondents

Sl. No.		Rayala Seema Backward Caste				Telangana Backward Caste				Andhra Backward Caste			
		A	B	C	D	A	B	C	D	A	B	C	D
1.	Cat-A	38 (61.29)	8 (14.81)	5 (9.26)	14 (37.84)	7 (18.92)	8 (21.62)	6 (16.22)	9 (36.00)	7 (28.00)	7 (26.92)	6 (15.00)	12 (37.58)
2.	Cat-B	11 (17.74)	13 (24.07)	15 (27.78)	5 (13.51)	3 (8.11)	6 (16.22)	3 (8.11)	3 (12.00)	4 (16.0)	17 (65.38)	2 (5.00)	7 (18.42)
3.	Cat-C	9 (14.52)	12 (22.22)	19 (35.19)	7 (18.92)	12 32.43)	13 (35.14)	11 (29.73)	9 (36.00)	8 (32.00)	6 (23.08)	5 (12.50)	11 (28.95)
4.	Cat-D	4 (6.45)	21 (38.89)	10 (18.52)	11 (29.73)	15 (40.54)	15 (40.54)	5 (13.51)	4 (16.00)	7 (28.00)	10 (38.46)	3 (7.50)	8 (21.05)
5.	Total	62 (100.00)	54 (100.000	49 (90.74)	37 (100.00)	37 (100.00)	41 (110.81)	25 (67.57)	25 (100.00)	26 (104.00)	40 (153.00)	16 (40.00)	38 (100.00)

Source: Compiled from the data collected from field work.

The finding of the table is that in the study area the people belonging to category 'A' and 'B' are the most affected people are the most benefited people and from the category 'C' and 'D'.

References

1. Singhi, N.K. *Bureaucracy, Positions and %* (New Delhi: Abhinav Publications, 1974), p. 55.
2. Sashilata Puri, *Legislative Elite in an Indian State: A Case Study of Rajasthan* (New Delhi: publications, 1978), p. 31.
3. Geraint Parry, *Political Elites* (London: George Allen and Unwin Ltd., 1969), p. 264.
4. Kiran Saxena, *Women and Politics*, Gyan Publishing House, New Delhi, 2000, p. 87.
5. Anil Kumar Singh, *Approach to Tribal Development*, Sarup and Sons, New Delhi, 1994, p.123.
6. Lipset, S.N., *The Political Man: The social basis of politics* (London: Heineman, 1960), p. 264.

Chapter - VII

Conclusion

The statement of the problem of the present study entitled **"POLITICAL PROCES OF BACKWARD CASTES (BCs) IN PANCHAYAT RAJ INSTITUTIONS (PRIs): PROS AND CONS - A STUDY IN ANDHRA PRADESH"** covers various discriminations the Panchayat raj institutions in Andhra Pradesh. The PRIs in Andhra Pradesh evolved due to the recommendations of various study teams, the amendments of constitution and the acts of central and state governments. This chapter presents precise summary about all has done and found in the present study. The thesis comprises of seven chapters in all.

The first chapter is introduction, an attempt is made to discuss about the panchayat raj institutions and political participation of backward castes.

Without understanding the Indian society, its nature - social structure, pattern of land holding, caste structure, the problem of rural villages, it may not be possible to understand the working of rural local Governments in India. Since Indian society is based on caste system and consequent social inequality, only the people from higher social status used to be involved in the process of administration, directly or indirectly.

Social inequalities existed in the villages and these have continued for centuries. Under these circumstances, soon after Independence the concept of social justice figured in the Indian constitution. Thus, the constitution of India made an attempt to provide equal social opportunities for the development of personality of all the people in the society, without any discrimination on the basis of caste, sex or race.

However, social inequalities continued for a long time in the Indian society. The reasons may be several. The people from higher social strata had received education, and they controlled and managed land. They took up income - earning activities. On the contrary, the lower strata people were denied education, and they were deprived of their right to manage and control land. Thus, they were forced to take up low - income earning activities. Particularly in the villages the lower strata people took up supportive works for the people who had taken up agricultural activities, such as Carpentry, Blacksmith, Leather work, and labour.

Due to the above-mentioned reasons the marginalised became the weaker sections of the society. Therefore, after Independence, India was one among the countries which went in for social and economic transformation of the rural population. As a preferred condition, rural development became a definite strategy for the improvement of the living conditions of the rural poor. In this direction the Government of India made efforts to solve problems such as poverty, ill health, illiteracy, and backwardness of varied nature prevailing in rural areas, by giving greater attention to the uplift of the rural poor.

Further, the marginalised sections, i.e., SC, ST, OBC have become an important component in defining of the development policies because of their socio-economic deprivation in the traditional society like India. The political involvement of the upper castes is still more in institutions like Assembly and Parliament. The reservation of seats was 15% in State Assemblies and Parliament. On the contrary there was no representation from the larger sections of the marginalised castes i.e., from the backwards. As a result of this, at present, political participation in India is limited to only a few upper castes. As they manage and control the political system, land pattern. The upper caste people did not mind in formulating and execution of welfare and developmental policies intended for the weaker sections. It can be seen in the failure of several programmes. Among these are Community Development Programmes (CDP) and National Extension Programme (NEP). These programmes were implemented in tune with the upper caste people in the rural areas.

Balwant Ray Mehta Committee Report

In 1957, under the chairmanship of Balwant Ray Mehta a study team was appointed. The purpose was to evaluate the functioning of CDP. While reviewing the functions of CDP Balwant Ray Mehta committee thought about panchayat raj system. Thus, the creation of panchayat raj system in India is purely by the intellectual contribution of Balwant Ray Mehta committee. The creation of panchayat raj system was begun in India on 2nd October 1959 in Rajasthan, Andhra Pradesh, Tamil Nadu, Kerala, Madhya Pradesh, Orissa, Uttar Pradesh, Bihar, West Bengal, Himachal Pradesh, Gujarat, Assam, and in some union territories. The basic purpose of creating the panchayat raj system is purely to meet the local problems and to implement the developmental programmes. Balwant Ray Mehta committee recommended three tier system for panchayat raj. The committee gave the thrust on panchayat Samithi, which is to be established at block level. It is known as block level body. It is a statutory and executive body, comprehensive in its functions, equipped with necessary authority and in possession of adequate resources. The committee further felt that the Panchayat Samithi must not be cramped by too much control by the government agencies. It is an important to note that the committee had given importance to panchayat samithi and neglected the other two systems of PRI's. Among the other reasons the most important reason was that the committee wanted to implement rural developmental programmes very effectively and without interference from political parties and groups.

Ashok Mehta Committee

An important committee which was appointed in 1977 by the new government at the center was Ashok Mehta committee. It was appointed to enquire into the working of PRI's and suggest measures to strengthen them to "enable a decentralised system of planning and development to be effective". The committee also suggested recommendations only with the intention of development in rural areas. It recommended reform and revitalisation of panchayat raj based upon the central premises of "linking institutions of democratic decentralisation with socially motivated economic development".

Both the acts thought of attempting to bring about rural development either by three or two tier system of panchayat raj institutions. They could not achieve the specified motive to a larger extent, due to the ignorance of the people, non-involvement of weaker sections, to whom the schemes are to be reached. The upper caste and dominant people of the villages intentionally diverted the schemes. Thus, the attempt of panchayat raj institutions in developing the weaker sections has remained limited only to the records.

In view of these, the constitutional amendment Act of 1992 was came into enforce in the year 1993 known as 73rd Constitutional Amendment Act of 1993. As per the Act, a due share has been provided to the social groups that is OBCs for their political participation and to take up plans and programmes for the welfare of these sections. The 73rd Amendment Act on the other side opted several opportunities only to the people with better agrarian resources among BCs. Thus, the developmental programmes are not reaching to the lower strata categories among BCs and still they remain backward.

Origin of the Problem

The lines of exploitation in pre-British India, in terms of the production, extraction and accumulation of surplus, were structured through the caste system. This identified a particular caste division of labour involving specific forms of hierarchy among the exploited, with at least three major groups identified in most villages: toiling peasant castes, most of whom were simply cultivators but with some village management powers held by a dominant lineage, artisans and service castes performing particular caste-duties within a *jajmani* system: a large caste of general labourers working for the village and its dominant sections and classes as 'untouchable'. Tribals and pastoralists outside the village were also among the exploited sections. The exploited as a whole included a very wide range of castes, the broad 'toiling caste majority'.

The toiling caste majorities also known as the backward classes, which is a general term applied to three different categories of people who have been identified, they are the scheduled castes, scheduled tribes and other backward castes, which together constitute about one-third of the total population of India. Among three, the other backward castes constitute, in terms of numerical strength and castes, more. The term other backward classes was widely used by the British administration come to mean 'Other Backward Castes' in administrative usage. It is used in the Constitution of India to designate backward classes other than the scheduled castes and scheduled tribes. Article 15 (4) refers to them as 'socially and educationally backward classes (SEBC) of citizens' and Article 340 as 'socially and educationally backward classes'. Article 16 (4) mentions 'backward class of citizens' and Article 46 refers to 'the educational and economic interests of the weaker sections of the people'. No doubt, the constitutional recognition of the other backward classes as a category of public policy made it one of an all -India scope but by contrast it is a more nebulous category. The other backward classes were mentioned in the constitution in general terms. There were no all-India lists drawn for the other backward classes. They were not separately enumerated in the Constitution, and in fact, one has to work with only a rough estimate of their population. Their position was sought to be defined in more specific terms by the backward classes commission.

The Other Backward Castes also termed as backward classes in the policy matter and bureaucratic circles is having theoretical limitation. In fact, in the Indian context all the forward castes and *dalits* have got the class character due to their privileged and underprivileged social and economic position, therefore, they may be characterised as the upper class and lower class or exploiting class and exploited class. The backward castes also come under the exploited category by the upper caste but in a different form. The backward castes are collectively exploited and deprived all the privileges along with *dalits.* But untouchability is not practiced in the case of backward castes. For practicing the traditional caste based occupations to provide goods and services to the rulers in particular and mass in general got the higher position than the dalits and lower position than the upper castes and they are highly heterogeneous and stratified with similar socio-economic backwardness and interdependence nature of all these occupational castes. The traditional occupation prevented them to come out of the social stranglehold resulting in continued backwardness. Therefore, instead of calling them as backward classes, it would be more appropriate to term them as the 'Backward Castes'.

Political Participation

"Political participation" is a term having many meanings. It is applied to the activity of ordinary citizens and to the activity of political leaders. It is used to refer to many different kinds of activity: voting, campaign contributions, marching in May Day or Patriots' Day parades. A term so broad can lose its usefulness. We must begin, therefore, by defining and delimiting the meaning of political participation. It is not our purpose to present the definition of participation. We simply wish to clarify how we shall be using the term. This is the crucial first step in our analysis. The rest of this book shall be devoted to describing who participates in what way, and to explaining why they do so. But we first must understand what it is we are explaining. For this purpose, it is not enough to define participation; we must also discuss how to measure it, since our analysis requires that we be able to say *how* active a particular individual or group is.

The problem of defining and measuring political participation is compounded by the cross-national nature of our work. We shall be comparing participation across a heterogeneous set of nations. Is there something called political participation that can be meaningfully compared across these nations? And can we measure such activity in ways that are comparable enough to allow parallel analyses in each of the nations? Before we proceed, we must face these issues.

What is political participation?

By political participation, we refer to those legal activities by private citizens that are more or less directly aimed at influencing the selection of governmental personnel and/or the actions they take, though this is a rough definition. It is adequate for delimiting our sphere of interest. It indicates that we are basically interested in *political* participation, that is, in acts that aim at influencing *governmental* decisions. Ours is a broad conception. We are interested in a wide variety of ways in which citizens participate in relation to varied issues. Many studies of participation focus on the vote. Sometimes by choice, sometimes by default (because other data are not available), voting turnout of participation and for comparison with participation, not as measures of participation.

In addition, we limit our attention largely to participation vis-à-vis the government. The argument has been made that effective participation depends upon opportunities to participate in other spheres – family, school, voluntary associations, the workplace. A participatory polity may rest on a participatory society (Almond and Verba, 1963; Eckstein, 1961). We do not quarrel with this assumption. But we shall not attempt to describe and explain patterns of participation outside those that are more narrowly *political* – that is, aimed at affecting the government.

One last limitation in our focus is our concern with activities "within the system" – with "regular" and legal ways of influencing politics. This eliminates from our span of concern a wide range of acts – protests, riots, assassinations, all kinds of civil violence – through which private citizens might try to influence the government. This is not to argue that the latter is insignificant or unworthy of study. It is simply another topic. The activities with which we deal represent a set distinctive enough in origin and impact to merit separate consideration.

Review of Related Literature

Various research studies have been conducted to study the women, SC, ST, BC's leadership at Panchayat level in different states. The Panchayat elections that took place in the State of Madhya Pradesh in 1994, brought forward a large number of women, many of who belong to the Scheduled Castes and Scheduled Tribes and backward castes, besides male members. The studies on political participation of weaker sections in the institutions of PRIs in India have attracted the attention of scholars from defferent disciplines such as Political Science, Sociology, Economics and Women's Studies. An array of scholarly works examining the weaker section's representation, their nature, the factors contributing for their success and for failure along with policy implications has been brought out. A review of certain important works is quite pertinent in the context of the present study.

The review of some of such literature related to the topic are G. Palanithurai's (Ed.) *'Empowering People'* throws light on Panchayat Raj system, Panchayat Raj Movement and the status of Panchayat Raj system in India under various stages of innovations. *'Decentralisation and Local Politics'* edited by S.N. Jha and P.C. Mathur, deals Panchayat Raj System in India in general and gives us a knowledge about reforms, development of Panchayat Raj and its governance and the implications in scheduled areas P.C. Mathur in his book, *'Political Dynamics of Panchayat Raj'*, deals in length about Panchayat Raj system in India from 1959-90. Adhishesiah (Ed.) in his *'Need for Constitutional Safeguards in Panchayat Raj in Karnataka today: Its National Dimensions'*, dealt in detail about introduction of Panchayat Raj system, its effects and need for constitutional safeguards in Karnataka. Eminent experts in the field like B.S. Bhargav, C.R. Bada, and V.N. Toragal, regarding Panchayat Raj System (Karnataka) dealt with introduction, stages of growth, working and position of Panchayat Raj System in Karnataka, in general. 'The Power to the People' reflects Panchayat Raj Institution in Karnataka published by Department of Rural Development and Panchayat Raj, Government of Karnataka.

Sweta Mishra (1989), in her book *"Democratic Decentralisation"* reveals that, decentralisation is an ideological principle associated with objectives of self-reliance, democratic decision-making, popular participation in governmental affairs and accountability of public servants to the citizens. Decentralisation is essential to achieve the broad political objectives such as, promoting political stability, mobilising support and co-operation for development policies and providing heterogenous regions, interests and communities, with a task in the survival of the political system.

Verma (1990), in his article "State Autonomy and Democratic Decentralisation", expressed doubts about the sincerity and faith of the central and state leaders in the philosophy of decentralisation. He regrets that states have been fighting with the center for more and more powers and autonomy and that too discretionary powers, not for democratic decentralisation but for enjoying and exercising more powers. Political leaders of the states have shown little concern over their own village folk. They have never realised the powerful heads, their existence role and importance of these local bodies. It has also been suggested by another writer that political leaders use these local leaders only as their vote-contractors and brokers. It has also been suggested by another writer that political leaders at the higher level must have deep rooted faith and reliance in the capacity and right of the rural masses. No one should consider them as unit for self-government on account of their poverty, illiteracy, ignorance, sex, language, religion and other forms and backwardness.

Nagendra Ambedkar (2000), in his book on *"Panchayat Raj at Work"*, explained the origins and growth of panchayat raj institution in India and structural patterns of panchayat raj in Rajasthan. The author also has given importance to electoral system of the local bodies. Further, he analyzed the socio-economic and political background of the panchayat raj elite, their perceptions and orientations of various issues, pertaining to the panchayat raj institution, finally he analyzed the leadership in panchayats and the qualities, attitude of the leaders towards weaker sections of the society.

Malviya (1956), in his book *"Village Panchayat in India"*, explains the historical and ideological background of the gram panchayats in India from times immemorial. The author focuses as to how the village panchayats in this ancient country developed into a sound system of democracy in accordance with our indigenous traditions and culture. The author concludes with a suggestion that the village panchayats are not the relic of tribalism or feudalism but are the results of matured experiment.

Significance of the Study

The study had a vast significant interims of understanding the political process of Backward Castes (BCs) in Panchayat Raj Institutions and its pros and cons in the state of Andhra Pradesh, where the agrarian structure, economic sources are being controlled by major communities. As these major land owning communities and other occupants of important positions of villages traditionally controlling the village politics for centuries. The purpose of the study is to understand the impact of reservation provisions for BCs in PRIs and the role of BCs in achieving the welfare of BCs in a caste dominated society. There are three categories of social groups resulted by rituals, economy and occupation. As a result of traditional occupation the lower social group was formed, because they are engaging in less income activities and living in chronic poverty. They are backward in terms of educationally, socially, economically and culturally. Under the circumstances the present study has its relevance to assess the nature of BCs with in categories are working in PRIs in Andhra Pradesh. It is also intended to examine whether the reservation provisions of 73rd amendment act really utilised by appropriate or genuine social groups among BCs in the state of Andhra Pradesh. It is to assess whether the positions in PRIs are captured by agrarian, economically dominated groups among BCs. The study is also intends to examine the role of caste and its dominance in political process of BCs in general and in the institutions of panchayat raj in particular. The focus of the study is to assess the conditions of BC's representatives in issues relating to faction, crime, economic conditions and related issues after 1994. Besides, its attempt to examine the merits and demerits of panchayat raj acts in terms of extending reservation provisions to people belonging to BCs along with policy implications.

The above mentioned studies have their relevance as well as importance, based on the objectives and type of research work they carried out. Besides all these studies , the present study is entirely different from the other studies as it is taken up in order to examine the nature of representatives among BCs are capturing positions of PRIs, in respect objectives, scope and methodology employed in the present study. Hence, the present study is one of the interdisciplinary one and has national and international status.

Objectives of the Study

The study has the following objectives:

- To assess the representation of backward castes in the institutions of PRIs in relation to social background in the three regions of Andhra Pradesh.
- To examine the welfare of backward categories with the political participation of representatives belonging to backward categories across the regions of Andhra Pradesh.
- To examine the pros and cons of reservation provisions to backward categories after 73rd amendment act in the three regions of Andhra Pradesh.
- To examine the factors determining for the involvement of BCs in PRIs in the three regions ofAndhra Pradesh.
- To assess the role of caste, social status and agrarian resources to capture various positions in institutions of Panchayat raj in the three regions of Andhra Pradesh.
- It is to assess the response of dominant castes towards the representatives of backward castes in the three regions of Andhra Pradesh.
- To examine the nature of political process of backward categories among the BCs through the PRIs.
- To assess the economic, crime and faction status of the families of representatives of BCs in PRIs in districts of Rayalaseema.

- To examine whether people belonging to higher social categories within backward castes are capturing the positions in PRIs or low social categories.
- To find out the reasons why the people belonging to lower social categories among backward castes are not capturing the various positions in PRIs across the regions of Andhra Pradesh.
- To recommend policy implications for achieving social justice by providing opportunities to the people belonging to lower social and economic categories in the three regions of AP.

Hypotheses

The study have the following Hypotheses:

- The reservation benefits in PRIs have reached only the dominant social categories among the BCs in Andhra Pradesh.
- The representatives belonging to BCs in panchayat raj institutions in the three regions of Andhra Pradesh are being controlled by upper caste people.
- The developmental programmes in PRIs are being utilised by the people belonging to higher economic groups among BCs.
- In Rayalaseema region representatives from BCs are involving in factions in the process of political participation and for their survival.
- The reservation benefits of 73rd amendment act have not reached to people belonging to lower castes among BCs.

Methodology

The aim of the study is to assess the status of backward castes with reference to the nature of social categories among the BCs. The important focus of the study is to identify the factors affecting the really backward categories in political process in the institutions of panchayat raj. The aim of the study is also to assess the impact of social status (caste) in the political process of BCs in particular and in the working of PRIs in general. The study is to examine the social, economic and crime status of families of representatives in PRIs in regions of Rayalaseema. As the study intends to examine which categories from BCs are capturing the positions in PRIs by the reservation provisions and finally to evaluate the over all benefits of welfare policies whether reached to the needy people from BCs or not. For this purpose an Analytical, Descriptive and Normative methods have been employed in the study.

Research Design

As the study is to be conducted in the three regions of Andhra Pradesh and the purpose of the study is to find out whether the positions in PRIs are being captured by higher social categories with better agrarian resources among BCs after 73rd amendment act. It is to suggest the policy implications for the political participation of lower strata categories among BCs in PRIs in the three regions of Andhra Pradesh. For this purpose the required data for the present study has been conducted randomly with the help of stratified random technique. The proposed study was conduced in the three regions of Andhra Pradesh viz., Telangana, Andhra and Rayalaseema, two Mandals from each district were chosen taking in to consideration of literacy, unemployment, nature of caste among BCs and their population, social and development indicators in-depth analysis of representation of BCs was made. The factors affecting for non-involvement of people from lower social categories among BCs in the institutions of panchayat raj were also examined. For suggesting policy implications opinions were elicited from the different sections of people using scientific research techniques in the three regions of Andhra Pradesh.

Sourcess of Data

In order to conduct the proposed study the required information will be conducted from both primary and secondary sources. The macro aspect of the study will be based on the published and unpublished works on the subject, reports of panchayat raj institutions along with government. Exclusively in this study records, reports, annual action plans, budgetary documents, schemes of zilla panchayats and Mandal Panchayats prepared in different districts, district statistics, documents of PRIs in defferent districts were the main sources of data. The uses of websites such as www.Ap.nic.in, Andhra Pradesh .com, localgovernmentindia.org, censusindia.com and other leafleted web services were also be used for collecting primary and secondary data. Secondary data was also collected from books, journals and newspapers. In addition to these sources, primary information has been collected through interview scheduled intended to serve to a cross-sections of representatives, officials, caste leads from BCs were used for analysis. The collected primary is 450 in total, which represents 150 from each study area i.e. 150 from Anantapur district, 150 from Warangal district and 150 from East Godawari district.

Techniques of Data Collection and Analysis

In view of the objectives, need and importance of the present study, the required data has been collected using different methods of scientific techniques. Particularly, different methods of social enquiry were adopted. A special tool (questionnaire) was used by the investigator using the scientific process. The questionnaire consists of items in all spared over behaviour areas and also to collect the personal data i.e., name, sex, age, social, economic, political and educational background. Further, the collected data has been analyzed with the help of computer. It was transformed in to computer code and analysis was made with the help of single variable or multivariable tables. Statistical tools such as average, percentage, mean, correlation, cross-sectional and SES has been measured.

In the second chapter an attempt is made to elaborately discuss the Evolution of Panchayat Raj system in India.

The focus is given to discuss the Evolution of Panchayati Raj system in ancient India, medieval period and British period. It also considers in short the glimpses of development of Panchayati Raj system after independence.

Evolution of Panchayati Raj System in Ancient India

Panchayati Raj is not a new concept to India. Panchayats have been a part of rural cultural heritage of India. From time immemorial, panchayats have enjoyed the confidence of the people. The system has survived in spite of turmoils and changes, because the village folk were fully confident of their own capabilities of sound thinking and right approach to their problems.

Panchayat literally means an assembly (yat) of five (panch) wise and respected elders chosen and accepted by the village community. They were considered as the incarnation of God (panch parameshwar). Panchayats had a wide spectrum of activities covering executive, administrative, developmental and judiciary. They breathed health into the rural society.

Villages of Ancient India

The autonomous village is best described by Sir Charles Metcalf: The village communities are little republics, having nearly everything they can want within themselves. Dynasty after dynasty tumbles down; revolution succeeds revolution, but the village community remains the same. This union of village communities, each one forming a separate little state in itself, has contributed more than any other to the cause of the preservation of the people of India and the enjoyment of freedom and independence.

In ancient India people were living in joint families. The patriarch of the joint family wielded very wide powers over its members. A federation of such small families were living in a village. The seniormost member of the seniormost family in the village was regarded with great reverence by the village community and was entrusted with the governmental functions.

The institutions of joint family thus gradually led to the evolution of kingship. Since ancient times, the village has been the unity of administration. Its importance was naturally very great in an age. When the means of communications and transport was slow and raids were frequent. Villages in ancient India were productive and prosperous and as such their importance in a state or kingdom was very significant. Vedic hymns frequently prayed for the prosperity of villages. Kings like Bimbisara used to convene a meeting of village headmen to discuss important questions of administrative policy.

Dr. Altekar sums up aptly that, "There is no doubt that villages were the real centres of social life and important units in the country's economy. They sustained the edifice of national culture prosperity and administration".

India has been the cradle of rural local government which continued to flourish from the time of Vedic civilisation to the advent of British rule. In the Indian history the village was the basic unit of Government, whether the central authority was monarchical or republican. The rural local government is the very foundation stone on which every empire in India has been reared. The village in India has been considered as the basic unit of the local self administrations since Vedic times.

The village has been the mainstay of rural India throughout the countries. The term for the village was the "grama" "ksetra" and "usvara" which from Rig Vedic denoted plough land. The villages were prosperous the Gramik or Gramini and other village elders were responsible for village defence. There was little interference by the state in their activities.

The village communities were always self-sufficient, self-reliant and independent.

The village administration was carried on under supervision and direction of the village headmen. Verilly called grama or gramika or grameyaka in northern India, munuda in the eastern deccan, gramukata, or govunda in Karnataka and Mahattaka or Mahantaka in the U.P.

References to such a highly organised system of local government can also be found in the Vedas, in the Epics - of Ramayana and Mahabharatha, Manusmriti, in the literature of Buddhist and Jains and in Koutilyas *Arthashastra*. The Vedas (Rig Veda in particular) reveal that prime used to live in small traditional guilds; which where generally controlled and regulated by popular institutions.

The control of the state over the village continued to be mentioned in the later days of the Manusmriti in which the king used to place a company of soldiers, commanded by a trusted official, in the midst of two, five or hundreds of villages. The king was empowered to appoint a lord for each village as well as a lord for ten villages (Deshi).

During the period of Buddhism and Jainism villages were classified according to the size and mode of habitation. The villages were self sufficient and self dependent. The village headmen was known as Bhojak. His duty was to collect the revenue for the state and to organise the constructive programmes. The Bhojak was selected by the villagers on the basis of local customs and traditions.

During the rule of Mouryan Emperors, the process of village administration underwent some changes. Under Chanakya's rule villages were classified according to the population. The village administration during this period (324-236 BC) was closely linked with agriculture. The size of the village varied from 100 to 500 families. The following officials composed the village administrative staff.

1. The headman (Adyaksha).
2. The accountant (Samkhayaka).
3. The village officials of different grades (Sthanikas).
4. The village countries (Jamgha karika).
5. Veterinary Doctor (Anikartha).
6. Village Medical Officer (Chikitska).
7. Horse trainer (Ashwa Damok).

The above mentioned members of assembly were not elected but they were chosen by a sort of natural selection. The headman was the president of the village assembly and its executive official. He was the leader of the village both for civil purposes and for military operations. The members of assembly were wholly responsible for the service of the community in their respective fields.

During the times of Harsha in the sixth century these panchayats were active. There were panchayats for different occupational ground and one for the village as a whole during the post-Mouryan period from 200 BC to 300 AD known as the "Dask period" the village continued to be smallest unit of the administration. The headman assisted by the council of elders, still played a prominent role in village life. The village under the Mouryan period was efficiently organised. The traditional elders found that the system and concepts of programmes of the Vedic age were still dominant, was also a feature of Gupta's rule.

The system did not change under the imperial Guptas, although it underwent certain changes in nomenclature. The district official was known as "Vishayapathi". He was a feudatory Maharaja owing allegiance to the emperor and enjoying autonomy in regard to internal matters. He was advised, by guild presidents, chief scribes and leading persons of locality. The villagers were governed by Gramapati (headman) assisted by the village assemblies. The assembly consisted of entire population of the area. The male adults and some times Mahattaras (a body of selected elders). The assembly appointed a number of committees to look after the various aspects of village administration.

The village officers consisted of headman, accountant, watchman, school teacher, priest, supervisor of irrigation works and boundary man. All of them were paid according to the local customs either in the form of a grant of rent free land or share of crop at the harvesting time. The village had its own funds. The inference of police officials of the mining department was permitted in special cases but they were very rare.

Thus, in ancient India rural local government was omni-competent, financially viable, practically autonomous and imbued with a gracious civic spirit. It was frictionless machine and characterised by the high degree of efficiency, impartiality and integrity. The panchas has a sense of dedication to the service of the people who had both a sense of involvement and a feeling of independence.

Medieval India

A new chapter of Indian history and culture begins with the arrival of Muslims in India. The first Muslims who came to India were Arabs who conquered Sindh and Multan in 712 A.D. With the passage of time, the much-cherished independence of the village bodies began to diminish during the Muslims; particularly the Mughal rulers ultimately succeeded Hindu Rajas. The earlier districts and villages were put under the charge of the centrally appointed subedars, amatyagars, muqaddams and patvaris. The pattern of village local government however continued practically unaltered, thus keeping up the tradition of continuity of local government till the advent of British Raj.

Hugh Tinker says that, "The Mughals had interfered very little with the ancient customs of village government. They incorporated the village into the administration as a unit for revenue and police purposes only. The state through the headman or muqaddam who was held responsible for the maintenance of law and order and the restriction of their within that area of his authority. The Judicial powers of the village council, the panchayat were considerably curtailed, under the mughals, otherwise the local affairs remained unregulated from above and the village officers and servants were answerable primarily to the panchayats".

Though Muslim rulers did not interfere with the working of local institutions very much, still due to the strict bureaucracy, the cultivators had to suffer very much in closing years of Shah Jahan's rule, in fact, these nobles became more democratized, the peasants were more harassed by the provincial government, their condition deterioted and the evil of pauperism increased.

The villages lost all powers and the village assembly had no influence. There was no direct relationship between the villagers and the state. No attention was paid to the development of local institutions. But Akbar the great, was an exception who reorganised the whole revenue system by establishing direct relations of state with the cultivators. The village headsman that was known as Choudhari, or Mukhiya or Muqaddam, was treated as village servant and responsible for the public works. This muqaddam was the main link between the government and the village. The government dealt with the peasants through him. It may be presumed that the village headman was the most important individual in the general economy of village.

In the third chapter working of panchayat raj system in Andhra Pradesh is discussed.

One of the tasks of nation building and development, writes Milton J. Esman is to bring members of the national community into a network of relationships and institutions which enable them to participate actively in decisions affecting their individual and group welfare while this is true of all nations, it has posed a considerable problem to the developing nations like India.

The principle that members of the national community should have an opportunity to participate actively in decisions affecting their lives is accepted by most of the persons charged with the responsibility of shaping the policies. In this context Panchayati Raj as a system of rural local administration has come a long way since its inception in the late 1950s as a corrective to the lapse noted in the working of the bureaucratically dominated community development programme initiated in the early 1950s as a corrective to the lapse noted in the working of the bureaucratically dominated community development programme initiated in the early 1950s. An organically linked-up three-tier system of village panchayats. Panchayat samithis and Zilla Parishad was installed in quick succession in several states as a sequel to the recommendation of Balwant Ray Mehta study team report of 1957. With the introduction of the panchayati Raj institutions there was a shift from bureaucratic administration to democratic administration. The idea of adopting this system was to have a democratic approach and to place the administration in the hands of both the officials and elected representatives so as to make them partners in the development process. This was a new experiment in the sphere of rural local government administration. The system formulates and executes development programmes through people's participation and instills political consciousness among the rural people. These Panchayati Raj institutions emerged as the institutions of socio-economic, political and cultural development with the provision of effective people's participation in policy formulation and implementation at the grassroots level.

Andhra Pradesh is one of the first two states in the country to establish the Panchayati Raj set-up in 1959 much on the lines of the Balwant Ray Mehta Committee Report. The experience of Panchayati Raj in Andhra Pradesh is nearly three and a half decades old during this period, the Government of Andhra Pradesh appointed several commissions and committees and made attempts to improve the functioning of the Panchayati Raj have become moribund (and) they have been denuded of their promise and vitality. The committee felt that the institutions of Panchayati Raj have to be viewed as institutions of self-government which would naturally facilitate the participation of the people in the process of planning and development flowing from and as a part of the concept of self government. This committee reiterated the conceptualisation of Panchayats embodied in Article 40 of the constitution. The committee recommended that "local self government should be constitutionally recognized, protected, preserved by the inclusion of a new chapter in the constitution".

In conformity with the Constitution 73rd Amendment Act, 1992 the Andhra Pradesh Legislature enacted the Andhra Pradesh Panchayati Raj Act-1994. It repealed three of its earlier Acts relating to the Panchayats Act, 1964, Andhra Pradesh Mandal Praja Parishad, Zilla Praja Parishad and Zilla Pranalika and Abhivrudhi Mandals Act 1986 and Andhra Pradesh Local Bodies Electoral Reforms Act, 1989.

Thus, the new Act reintroduced a three tier system of Panchayati Raj constituting Zill Parishads (ZPs) at the district level, Mandal Parishads (MPs) at the intermediary level and Gram Panchayat (GPs) at the village level by merging the Andhra Pradesh Gram Panchayats Act, 1964 and Andhra Pradesh Abivrudhi and Sameseeksha Mandals Act, 1986.

The present pattern of Panchayati Raj in the state is functioning under the Andhra Pradesh Panchayati Raj Act 1994. Keeping in view the past experiences it became imperative to provide constitutional status to local self-government to impart certainty, continuity and strength. The Constitution's 73rd Amendment essentially lays down certain ground values with basic structural framework so that it can sustain against external interference and could establish themselves as effective and strong people's institutions.

The powers and functions of the Panchayati Raj institutions are on the lines of the 73rd Amendment Act. All the 29 items included in the Eleventh Schedule inserted by the 73rd Constitutional Amendment Act find a place in schedule I of the Andhra Pradesh Panchayati Raj Act, 1994. The subjects mentioned in schedule I of the Act are common to all the three tiers of the Panchayati Raj Institutions.

Structure of the Panchayati Raj System

Gram panchayat

Constitution of a Gram Panchayat

The Gram Panchayat is the body constituted for a village, the administration of a village is vested in Gram Panchayat, every Gram Panchayat is a body corporate by the name of the village with a perpetual succession and a common seal. As a corporate body it can sue and can be sued in a court of law. It can acquire and hold and transfer its property and can enter into contracts to discharge its duties under the Act.

The term of office of the Gram Panchayat is five years.

Strength of a Gram Panchayat

According to a provision of the Act "A Gram Panchayat shall consist of such number of elected members inclusive of its

Gram Panchayat with a population at the time of last Census	Number of members
(1)	(2)
Up to 300	5
Exceeding 300 but not exceeding 500	7
Exceeding 500 but not exceeding 1,500	9
Exceeding 1,500 but not exceeding 3,000	11
Exceeding 3,000 but not exceeding 5,000	13
Exceeding 5000 but not exceeding 10,000	15
Exceeding 10,000 but not exceeding 15,000	17
Exceeding 15,000	Between 19 and 21

Source: AP Panchayati Raj Act. 1994, p. 15.

Sarpanch as may be notified from time to time, by the commissioner, the number of members notified is shown in Table 7.1.

Election of Members

All members of the Gram Panchayat are elected by the registered voters in the ward by the method of secret ballot. The act has adopted two children norm as a qualification for the members of the panchayat. In addition, all other members except women who are absent for a period of ninety days from the date of the commencement of the term of office or absent for three ordinary meetings continuously are disqualified. In the case of women a period of not less than four months at a time is excluded if the lady is physically disabled or due to advanced stage of pregnancy and delivery.

Reservation of seats of members of Gram Panchayat

In every Gram Panchayat out of the total strength of elected members the seats are reserved to Scheduled Castes and Scheduled Tribes subject to the condition that the number of seats so reserved shall bear the same proportion to the total number of seats to be filled by the direct election to the Gram Panchayat. Such reserved seats for scheduled castes and scheduled tribes are allotted by rotation to different wards in a Gram Panchayat, besides, allotted by rotation to different wards in a Gram Panchayat. Besides, one-third of seats are reserved for women who include those belonging to scheduled castes and scheduled tribes based on their population ratio. The amendment No. 5, dated February 3rd, 1995 to the Act. Stipulated reservation of not less than thirty-four percent of the seats for the backward classes.

The Sarpach

Election and Term

The Sarpanch of the Gram Panchayat is directly elected by

the people enrolled in electoral rolls for the Gram Panchayat through the method of secret ballot on non-party basis. The election of the Sarpanch may be held at the same time and in the same place as the ordinary elections of the members of the Gram Panchayat as per the Act, the term of office of the Sarpanch who is elected at an ordinary election shall be five years from the date appointed by the election authority for the first meeting of the Gram Panchayat after the ordinary election[21]. Any casual vacancy in the office of the Sarpanch shall be filled within 120 days from the date of occurrence of such vacancy by a fresh election. And a person elected as Sarpanch in any such vacancy shall hold office only so long as the person in whose place he is elected would have been entitled to hold office if the vacancy had not occurred.

It is to be noted that no casual vacancy in the office of the Sarpanch shall be filled within six months before the date on which the ordinary election of the sarpanch shall be held[23] unless the competent authority (Commissioner appointed for that purpose under the Act) so directs. The Act clearly lays down that a person is not qualified to contest for the office of the Sarpanch, if he is less than 21 years of age; and if his name is not included in the electoral rolls of the village to which he contests. A person shall be disqualified for election as Sarpanch if he is in arrears of any dues, or is interested in a contract within the jurisdiction of the Mandal Parishad in which his village lies.

Reservation

The office of the Sarpanch is again reserved for different categories of people like Scheduled Castes, Scheduled Tribes, Women and Backward Classes on the scale of reservation adopted for electing the members.

Upa- Sarpanch

One of the persons is elected as the Upa-Sarpanch from amongst the members. When the office of the Sarpanch is vacant, the Upa-Sarpanch exercises the powers and performs the function of the Sarpanch until a new Sarpanch is elected and assumes office.

Powers and Functions of the Sarpanch

The Sarpanch has powers and functions specified by the Act, besides, the Sarpanch has the emergency powers.

The Sarpanch

(a) Is responsible for making arrangements to the election of the Upa- Sarpanch.

(b) Has access to the records of the gram panchayat.

(c) Exercise administrative control over the executive officer for the purpose of implementation of the resolutions of the Gram Panchayat or its committee.

(d) Has power to get information from any village secretary of any village within the jurisdiction of the Gram Panchayat.

(e) Is responsible for intimating to the District Panchayat Officer as to the disqualifications of the members of the panchayat.

(f) Acts within the resolution of the Gram Panchayat.

(g) Can devolve the powers and functions to Upa- Sarpanch as per the Act.

(h) Can direct any executive work of the gram panchayat in the interest of general public. However, he is required to inform the same to the gram committee in the ensuing meeting. This refers to the emergency powers of the Sarpanch.

In the fourth chapter an attempt is also made to analyze the profile of Andhra Pradesh the successful implementation of any development programme emphasizes the need for considering the resource base of a particular area. There is also direct correlation between the resource base and enlistment of the communities through various programmers since the available resources in the region have greater effect on the real development process of the area therefore it is more appropriate to project the study area for understanding its development potentials. The present chapter is accordingly focused on the study area and related aspects. The chapter briefly deals with the salient features of Andhra Pradesh and the study areas such as Anantapur district in Rayalaseema, Warangal in Telangana and West Godawari in Andhra Regions.

(a) THE STATE

Location

On 1st November 1956, the States Reorganisation Act merged the Telugu-speaking areas of the former Hyderabad state also known as Telangana with the Andhra state to form the state of Andhra Pradesh. The city of Hyderabad, the former capital of the Hyderabad State, was made the capital of the new state.

The state of Andhra Pradesh is located between 13° to 20° North latitude and 77° to 85° East longitudes. The state is bound by the Bay of Bengal on the East with a coastline of 974 kilometers, on its northeast by Orissa, in its North by Madhya Pradesh and Maharashtra in its West and Southwest by Karnataka and in its South by Tamil Nadu. Andhra Pradesh is the fifth largest state in the Indian union both in terms of area as well as population.

The state has area of 2.72 lahs sq.km forming 804 percent of total geographical area of the country. The state has the longest coastline (974 kms.) among all the littoral states in India.

Climate

The state has tropical to sub-tropical climate. Humid to semi-humid conditions prevail in the coastal area in the interiors of the state the climate is arid to semi-arid the interior plateau areas have hot summers with relatively pleasant winters. The state receives rainfall mainly from the Southwest monsoon (about 67 percent) and partly from the Northeast monsoon.

Rainfall

The average annual rainfall ranges from 650 mm in semi-arid belt to about 1300 mm in the North Western portion of the state. Rayalaseema region is a zone of low rainfall, recording an average rainfall of 1100 mm and the area north of the Godavari River receives 100-1300 mm of rainfall increases from Southwest of Northeast and also from West to East.

Temperature

The minimum and maximum temperatures of the state generally vary from 13.4°C to 19.7°C and 33.9°C to 42.8°C respectively regional variations in temperature are quite noticeable.

Soils

The state is endowed with a variety of soils ranging from highly fertile and productive deltaic alluvial to black soil and the red soils cover over 66 percent of the area in the Reyalaseema districts. These types of soils have a low nutrient content. The black soils cover another 25 percent found in the Telangana region. The alluvial loamy clay soils found in Krishna and Godavari deltas cover 5 percent of the land. The coastal sands occupy 3 percent. The lacerate soils constituting 1 percent are seen in only in certain pockets.

Demographic features

Population

Andhra Pradesh is the fifth largest state in the Indian Union. It is the largest among the states in the southern region in terms of area and population. The state has registered a growth rate of 24.2 percent in population between 1981 and 1991. Which is slightly higher than the National growth rate by 2001 as it is 13.86 percent. For the first time in the last four decades the population growth rate of the state has overtaken according to the 2001 census report. The population of Andhra Pradesh is 75,727,541 of which 55,223,944 resides in rural and 20,503,597 reside in urban areas. The urban population works out to 27.08 percent which the rural population out to 72.92 percent.

Population Density

The population density of the state are 242 persons per sq. km. (1991) is lower than the national average (276) and much less than the density in the other southern states like Tamil Nadu and Kerala. However, it increased to 275 persons per sq. km in 2001 within the state the coastal Andhar region has a higher population density while Rayalaseema Region is sparsely populated. Sex ratio is defined as the number of females per thousand male populations. The sex ratio in Andhra Pradesh was showing decreasing trend since 1951 till 1991. However, for the first time, sex ratio has increased from 972 in 1991 to 978 in 2001. The sex ratio in Andhra Pradesh is higher than the all-India figure, which is 933. However, the position of Andhra Pradesh is third among the four southern states i.e., after Kerala (1058) and Tamil Nadu (986). In Andhra Pradesh, the lowest sex ratio is registered in Rangareddi, Hyderabad and Anantapur, where as the highest sex ratio is registered in Nizamabad, Srikakulam and Vizianagaram. The female to male population ratio as per 1991 census is 972/1000(1981=975/1000) as against the National Average of 927/1000. The sex ratio at all-India level, according to 2001 census report, is 933, which is an improvement over the sex ratio of 927 at 1991.

Literacy

The most important characteristic of population is literacy

which is a pre-requisite for the over all development of the country, both socially and economically. The definition of "Literate" for census of India 2001 is the same as was adopted at 1991 census. A person is considered as literate if she/he is able to read and write with understanding in any language. One who can merely read but cannot write is not considered as literate. However, to qualify as a literate it is not necessary that a person should have received any formal education. As in 1991 census all the children below 7 years of age have been treated as illiterates during census of India-2001. The literacy rate of Andhra Pradesh works out to 61.11 at 2001 as against 44.09 in 1991. The literacy rate for rural India is 55.33 in 2001 as against 35.74 in 1991. The literacy rate for urban India is 76.39 in 2001 as against 66.35 in 1991.

In the State of Andhra Pradesh among the districts Hyderabad is at the top with a literacy rate of 79.04 percent followed by West Godavari with 73.95 per cent, Krishna with 69.91 percent and Chittoor with 67.46 percent. The least literate district is Mahbubnagar with 45.53 percent followed by Vizianagaram with 51.82 percent and Medak with 50.24 percent. Among the rural population, West Godavari district ranks first in rural literacy rate with 72.48 percent followed by Krishna with 65.56 percent and Chittoor with 63.67 percent while least rural literacy was recorded in Mahbubnagar district with 46.86 percent (2001 Census Report).

Among the males, the literacy rate is 70.85 percent as against 51.17 percent among females as per 2001 census. Among the rural males the literacy rate is 66.13 percent as against 44.36 percent among the rural females. In totality, the literacy rate of Andhra Pradesh is lower than the all India literacy rate and difference in literacy rate between rural and urban and between male and female is very wide (2001 Census Report).

Rural population

Revenue villages together with hamlets, if any, constitute

the rural frame. There are 28,123 villages in Andhra Pradesh at 2001 as compared to 28,000 at 1991. The rural population accounts for 73.11 percent of the total population in the state as per 1991 census while the percentage of rural population is 72.92 percent as per 2001 census figures.

An attempt is made in the fifth chapter to elaborate portage the socio-economic background of the respondents.

In this chapter the political participation of backward castes in the institutions of panchayat raj has been analyzed on the basis of field experience. The field evidence with reference to the working of backward castes has been collected from the three districts i.e., Anantapur from Rayalaseema, Warangal from Telangana and East Godawari from Andhra Region and thus the collected data has been transformed in to computer and the respective tables are generated.

Table 7.1: District-wise Distribution of Respondents in Andhra Pradesh

Sl. No.	District	Frequency	Percentage
1.	Anantapur	150	33.33
2.	Warangal	150	33.33
3.	West Godavari	150	33.33
4.	Total	450	100.00

Source: Compiled from the data collected from field work.

Table 7.1 shows the district-wise distribution of sample respondents in the study area. It is observed from the table that the respondents have drawn from three district i.e., Anantapur district from Rayalaseema, Warangal from Telangana and West Godavari from Andhra region. The total respondents are 450, out of which 150 from each district.

Table 7.2 discusses the nature/type of members in the institutions of panchayat raj-wise distribution. The table reveals that the respondents' consists of chairman and vice-chairman are 3 with 0.67%, presidents of MPP are 21 with 5.33%, chairpersons of village panchayats are 45 with 10%, members of zilla panchayat are 60 with 13.33%, MPTC member are 60 with 13.33%, village panchayat members are 90 with 20% and the general public are 160 with 35.56%.

Table 7.2: Nature of Respondents

Sl. No.	Nature of Respondents	Frequency	Percentage
1.	Chairman/Vice-Chairman	03	0.67
2.	President MPP	24	5.33
3.	Chair Persons Village Panchayat	45	10.00
4.	Z P Members	60	13.33
5.	MPTC Members	60	13.33
6.	Village Panchayat Members	90	20.00
7.	General Public	160	35.56
8.	Total	450	100.00

Source: Compiled from the data collected from field work.

Table 7.3: Caste-wise Distribution of Respondents

Sl. No.	Caste	Frequency	Percentage
1.	Cat-A	125	27.78
2.	Cat-B	135	30.00
3.	Cat-C	90	20.00
4.	Cat-D	100	22.22
5.	Total	450	100.00

Source: Compiled from the data collected from field work.

Table 7.3 discusses the caste-wise distribution of respondents in the study area. The table reveals that the respondents belonging to category 'A' are 125 with 27.78%, from category 'B' are 135 with 30%, from category 'C' are 90 with 20% and from category 'D' are 100 with 22.22%.

The over all observation is that the higher social categorical among backward castes are more in the institutions of Panchayat Raj in Andhra Pradesh.

Table 7.4: Age-wise Distribution of Respondents

Sl. No.	Age	Frequency	Percentage
1.	18-25	116	25.78
2.	26-35	267	59.33
3.	36-45	59	13.11
4.	46-& Above	8	1.78
5.	Total	450	100.00

Source: Compiled from the data collected from field work.

Table 7.4 discusses the age-wise distribution of respondents. It is observed from the table that out of the total 450 respondents, the highest number 267 with 59.33% of respondents are from the age group of 26.35, followed by 116 respondents with 25.78% are from the age group of 18-25, 59 respondents with 13.11% are from the age group of 36.45 and the lowest number of respondents with 1.78% are from the age group of 46 and above.

The over all observation of the table is that there exists more number of respondents.

An attempt is also made in the sixth chapter to elaborate portage the awareness, perception and problems of political participation of backward castes.

It is widely believed that the analysis of age, education, caste, family structure, occupation, income, land holding, party affiliation, etc., are important in determining the nature of leadership. The data relating to socioeconomic background of elected respondents of Panchayati Raj Institutions were collected in the % study to get an insight into the emerging pattern of rural leadership in Anantapur, Warangal and East Godawari districts of Andhra Pradesh.

The socio-economic conditions play an important role in characterising the social life and behaviour of an individual. The socio-economic status of an individual affects the patterns of interaction in the society. It is therefore, essential to analyze the socio-economic background of the relationship between the leader and the environment. In a developing society like ours where forces of caste and kinship influence the social life and acute disparity in the standard of living and subculture among various groups and regions are existing[1], a study of the socio-economic conditions of OBC respondents would help reveal sociologically significant dimensions.

The socio-economic, educational and political background of the leaders would also enable us to anticipate as to what they are capable of doing, what we should expect from them and how well they are equipped to discharge the responsibilities developed upon them by the electorate.

Knowledge of socio-economic background of a community is an indispensable prerequisite, for the understanding of the thought or behaviours of its members. This holds good for all human communities, and more so in the case of SC/ST and OBC communities, which are intrinsically more traditional in their structure. As Geraint Parry observes: 'It is a widespread assumption of political sociology that social background and upbringing of a decision-maker will influence his attitudes and policies.

Table 7.5 discusses the caste-wise distribution of opinion toward the purpose of panchayat raj institutions. The opinion of backward caste in Rayalaseema shows that out of the total 62 belonging to category 'A' (62.90%) of the respondents are aware of the panchayat raj institutions. Followed by 66.67% belonging to category 'B', (53.06%) of respondents belonging to the category 'C' and 62.16% of respondents belonging to Category 'D'. And at the same time the highest number with 66.67% of respondents belonging to category 'B' are not aware of panchayat raj institutions.

In Rayalaseema, the most backward caste i.e., category 'A' and 'B' are participating in panchayat raj institutions.

The castes-wise opinion in Telangana reveals that the majority of the respondents belonging to category 'B' are participating in panchayat raj institutions. The majority of respondents i.e. 19 each from category 'A' and 'B' are not aware of the working of PRIs.

In the developed region of Andhra Pradesh, i.e., Andhra region, 29 respondents belonging to category 'B' and 22 respondents belonging to category 'D' are participating in PRIs. The table reveals that majority of respondents i.e. 16 belonging to category 'A' are not participating in the activities of PRIs.

The observation of the table is that among the backward castes, category 'A' and 'B' are more in Rayalaseema. Category 'B' people are more in Telangana and whereas in Andhra region category 'B' and 'D' are more in the activities of PRIs.

Table 7.6 discusses the caste-wise and region-wise distribution of opinion towards attending the grama sabha. The table reveals that Rayalaseema the majority of the respondents 38 and 30 belonging to category 'A' and 'B' are participating in the meetings of grama sabha. It is also identified that the majority 28 respondents belonging to category 'C' are not attending the meetings of gram sabha.

In Telangana region, majority of the respondents, 21 belonging to category 'B' and 17 respondents belonging to category 'D' are attending the meetings of gram sabha. The table also reveals that the lowest number of 8 and 11 respondents belonging to category 'C' and 'D' are not attending the meetings of grama sabha.

In Andhra region, the majority of respondents i.e., 27 belonging to category 'B' and 18 belonging to category 'D' are attending the meetings of grama sabha. 46.15% of respondents belonging to category 'A' and 32.50% of respondents belonging to category 'B' are not attending the meetings of grama sabha.

The over all findings of the table is that in Rayalaseema majority of people belonging to category 'A' and 'B' are attending the meeting of grama sabha. It is important to these

Table 7.5: Caste-wise Distribution of Opinion toward the Purpose of Panchayat Raj Institutions

		Rayala Seema Backward Caste				Telangana Backward Caste				Andhra Backward Caste			
		A	B	C	D	A	B	C	D	A	B	C	D
Sl. No.	Opinion	Frequ ency	Frequ-ency	Frequ-ency	Frequ-ency	Frequ-ency	Frequ-ency	Frequ-ency	Frequ-ency	Frequ-ency	Frequ-ency	Frequ-ency	Frequ-ency
1.	Yes	39 (62.90)	36 (66.67)	26 (53.06)	23 (62.16)	18 (48.65)	26 (63.41)	7 (28.00)	16 (64.00)	10 (38.46)	29 (72.50)	13 (81.25)	22 (57.89)
2.	No	23 (37.10)	19 (66.67)	23 (53.06)	14 (37.84)	19 (51.35)	19 (46.34)	5 (20.00)	10 (40.00)	16 (61.54)	6 (15.00)	6 (37.5)	15 (39.47)
3.	Total	62 (100.00)	54 (100.00)	49 (100.00)	37 (100.00)	37 (100.00)	41 (100.00)	25 (100.00)	25 (100.00)	26 (100.00)	40 (100.00)	16 (100.00)	38 (100.00)

Source: Compiled from the data collected from field work.

Table 7.6: Caste-wise and Region-wise Distribution of Opinion towards Attending the Grama Sabha

		Rayala Seema Backward Caste				Telangana Backward Caste				Andhra Backward Caste			
		A	B	C	D	A	B	C	D	A	B	C	D
Sl. No.	Opinion	Frequ ency	Frequ-ency	Frequ-ency	Frequ-ency	Frequ-ency	Frequ-ency	Frequ-ency	Frequ-ency	Frequ-ency	Frequ-ency	Frequ-ency	Frequ-ency
1.	Yes	38 (61.29)	30 (55.56)	21 (42.86)	25 (67.57)	16 (43.24)	21 (51.22)	17 (68.00)	14 (56.00)	14 (53.85)	27 (67.50)	10 (62.50)	19 (50.00)
2.	No	24 (38.71)	24 (44.44)	11 (22.45)	12 (32.43)	21 (56.76)	20 (48.78)	8 (32.00)	11 (44.00)	12 (46.15)	13 (32.50)	6 (37.50)	19 (50.00)
3.	Total	62 (100.00)	54 (100.00)	49 (100.00)	37 (100.00)	37 (100.00)	41 (100.00)	25 (100.00)	25 (100.00)	26 (100.00)	40 (100.00)	16 (100.00)	38 (100.00)

Source: Compiled from the data collected from field work.

that the majority of the rural development programmes is to be channalised and prepared through grama sabha. In Telangana and Andhra regions people belonging to category 'B' and 'D' are attending the meetings of grama sabha and participating in the development of grama panchayats.

In the seventh chapter is conclusion one, findings of the study and the policy implications are discussion. The study has the following findings:

1. The higher social categorical among backward castes are more in the institutions of panchayat raj in Andhra Pradesh.
2. There exists more number of respondents and representatives belonging to younger and middle age group.
3. The female respondents are more than 30 percentage.
4. An unmarried and divorced woman are also participating in the working of PRIs in the study area.
5. The respondents are from many religion background.
6. Nearly 85% of respondents are educated.
7. Majority of respondents, 300 with 68.66 percent are from agriculture and cooli background.
8. There exists more number of respondents with less income and the less number of respondents with higher range of income.
9. People with less number of acres of land and with low economic status only are participating in the working of panchayat raj institutions in the study area.
10. Majority of the respondents in the study area are depending on traditional modes of irrigation.
11. Among the backward castes, category 'A' and 'B' are more in Rayalaseema. Category 'B' people are more in Telangana and whereas in Andhra region category 'B' and 'D' are more in the activities of PRIs.

12. In Rayalaseema majority of people belonging to category 'A' and 'B' are attending the meeting of grama sabha. It is important to note that the majority of the rural development programmes is to be channalised and prepared through grama sabha. In Telangana and Andhra regions people belonging to category 'B' and 'D' are attending the meetings of grama sabha and participating in the development of grama panchayats.
13. Casteism and politics are the obstacles in the working of grama sabhas. It is also identified that the most backward castes are affected by casteism and faction and whereas the higher castes within OBCs are not participating due to politics and particularly by the involvement of lower castes. The lower castes are able to participate in PRIs only by the provisions of reservation to OBCs.
14. There exists more number of respondents belonging to category 'A' and 'B' and less number of respondents belonging to category 'C' and 'D' are asking questions in the meetings of grama sabhas.
15. The majority of the respondents belonging to category 'A' in all the three regions are not aware of powers of PRI's and the highest number of respondents belonging to category 'B', 'C' and 'D' in all the three regions are aware of power of panchayat raj institutions.
16. In all the three regions, the highest number of respondents belonging to category 'A' is not in a position of getting cooperation from the official working in the institutions of panchayat raj. It is also found that the majority of respondents belonging to category 'B', 'C' and 'D' in all the regions are getting cooperation from the officials in the institutions of panchayat raj.
17. The respondents belonging to backward categories in majority are exercising their franchise and there exists the political participation and process of backward castes.

18. The majority of the respondents belonging to category 'A' are not contesting the election in the institutions of panchayat raj. Whereas in Telangana and Andhra region the highest number of respondents belonging to backward castes are contesting the elections.
19. In Rayalaseema the majority of backward castes are not actively participating in the electoral process. Whereas in Telangana, except category 'A', other backward castes are actively participating in the elections. And in Andhra region the majority backward castes are actively participating in the elections.
20. The majority of respondents belonging to backward castes in Rayalaseema and Andhra region belonging to category A are not mobilising money during elections. In Telangana the majority of respondents are mobilising money during elections. In Andhra region respondents belonging to category 'B', 'C' and 'D' are mobilising money during elections. In Rayalaseema the backward castes political participation is controlled by the dominant Reddy and Kamma castes.
21. Respondents belonging to category 'A' in Rayalaseema, category 'B' in Telangana and category 'D' in Andhra region are not having any political affiliation to any political parties. On the other hand respondents belonging to category 'B', 'C' and 'D' in Rayalaseema, category 'A', 'C' and 'D' in Telangana and category 'A', 'B' and 'C' in Andhra region have political affiliation in different political parties. To understand the level of political participation and political process of the people can be understood and determine based on the level of political affiliation of the people.
22. Agricultural resources and numerical strength of the castes and also the social status of the caste within BCs

are the important factors to occupy the position in the institutions of panchayat raj.

23. In Rayalaseema and Telangana the people belonging to category 'C' are feeling that they are also belonging to upper castes and they do not have backward feeling. It is also observed from the table that in the study area, the upper castes belonging to category 'A', 'B' and 'D' feels that there is no unity among the backward castes and as a result they are not able to capture the political power in the institutions of panchayat raj institutions.
24. The weaker sections are not able to capture the political power due to illiteracy, low income and the dominance of upper castes.
25. In Rayalaseema, Telangana and Andhra region the reservation provision are not able to achieve the welfare of category 'A' and on the other hand able to achieve the welfare of category 'B', 'C' and 'D' people.
26. In all the regions the majority of respondents belonging to most backward categories are facing the criminal charges. The policy-makers have to think this aspect very seriously.
27. In all the three regions (study area). The present system of panchayat raj system has caused for the dominance of upper castes over the lower backward castes.
28. In the study areas, the upper caste people are supporting the people with higher social status within backward castes. It is the important findings of the study. The lower castes are not getting support from the forward castes and a result the upper castes within backwards are getting political positions.
29. In the study area the positions such as, ward member, presidents, MPTC, ZPTC and chairpersons from taluk and zilla panchayats under reserved categories for

backward castes are captured and controlled by the rich people within BCs. Though there is a reservation provisions for backward castes, economically poor people with in backwards are not able to enter in the institutions of Panchayat Raj institutions.

30. In the study area, the representatives are being elected with the caste composition and as a result they are extending their support to their caste people while implementing various developmental programmes.
31. There exist the caste based political representatives in the working of panchayat raj institutions. The people will get benefits of panchayat raj institutions if there is a representatives belonging to their caste.
32. In the study area the people belonging to category 'A' and 'B' are the most affected people are the most benefited people and from the category 'C' and 'D'.
33. In Rayalaseema, people belonging to Category A are more in PRIs. But they are also facing criminal cases, financial problems, threat to life, court cases.
34. In Telangana, people belonging to Category B and D are more in number and free from domination of upper castes.
35. In Andhra region people belonging to Category C and D are more in number and are more dominant.

The study has also the following policy implications:

Policy Implications

1. There should be internal reservation based on population within backward castes.
2. The lower castes such as Category A and B is to be given more preference as they are more in number and backward educationally, socially and politically comparatively to category C and D with in BCs.

3. Guidelines are to be framed for reaching Welfare policies and Developmental programmes people belonging to poor within BCs.
4. There should protection from the government to the representatives belonging to backward castes working in PRIs.
5. There should be financial remuneration and pension to the representative's belonging to backward castes working in PRIs.
6. If any charges or cases against representatives belonging to backward castes with political conspiracy the government has to extend legal aids.
7. There should be provision to attract the economically poor people within backwards.
8. Elections are to be conducted fairly and free.
9. The measures are to be taken for the involvement of weaker sections within BCs.
10. Measure is to be taken in order to exercise franchise.
11. Steps are to be taken for changing the mind set of upper caste people towards backwards.
12. It would be more relevance if reservation's priority given to most backward castes in PRIs.
13. The government has to create awareness among the people that the PRIs are only for the welfare of the poor people rather than political benefits.
14. Political participation of backward castes should be only for the implementation of welfare policies and development of BCs and should not be come mobiliser of votes.
15. Development is to be given more priority rather than political participation.
16. Weaker sections within OBCs, are to be given priority in the lines of proportional representation.

17. Identification of beneficiaries under any scheme should be from below poverty line.
18. Identification of beneficiaries under any scheme should be from appropriate beneficiaries.
19. Reservation provisions in PRIs should reach only the genuine persons.

Bibliography

Books

1. Atta Chand, *Panchayat raj and rural development*, Vol. III, Deep and Deep Publications, New Delhi, 1990.
2. Chatterjee, P, *The State and Politics in India*, Oxford University Press, New Delhi, 1997.
3. Cornwall, A, and Coelho, V. (eds.), *Spaces for Change? The Politics of Participation in New Democratic Arenas,* Zed Books, London, 2007.
4. Deshpande, Satish, 'Caste in equalities in India today' in H. S. Verma (Ed.): *The OBCs and the ruling classes in India (243-262).* Jaipur and New Delhi, Rawat Publication, 2005.
5. Dube, S.C, *Indian Villages*, Routledge, London (Reprint), 2002.
6. Dubey, S. N., *Administration of social welfare programmes in India*, Somiya Publications, New Delhi, 1973.
7. Engineer, Asghar Ali, *Mandal Commission controversy*, Ajanta Publications, New Delhi, 1991.
8. Fung, A, and Wright, E.O, *Deepening Democracy: Institutional Innovations in Empowered Participatory Governance,* Verso, London, 2003.
9. Goetz, A.M. 'Women's Political Effectiveness: A Conceptual Framework', in Goetz, A.M, and Hassim, S (eds) *No Shortcut to Power,* Zed Books, London, 2003.
10. Government of India, Report of the study team on social welfare and welfare of backward classes, 1958, manager of publications, Delhi, 1959.
11. Guijt, I, and Kaul Shah, M, *The Myth of Community*, IT Publications, London, 1998.
12. Gupta, D, 'Recasting Reservations in the Language of Rights', in Mahajan, G (ed.), *Democracy, Difference and Social Justice*, Oxford University Press, Delhi, 1998.
13. Hariss, J, Stokke, K, and Tornquist, O (eds) *Politicizing Democracy: Local Politics and Democratisation in Developing Countries,* Palgrave McMillan, London, 2005.

14. India, Government of study group on the welfare of weaker section. (Jaya Prakash Narayan: Chairperson) Report, Ministry of Community Development, New Delhi, 1970.
15. India, Government of working group on the empowerment of the other backward classes in the IX Five year plans (P. S. Krishna: Chairperson). Report: Planning Commission, New Delhi, 1997.
16. India, Government of Working group on the Empowerment of the other backward classes in the X Five year plan (P. S. Krishna: Chairperson) report, New Delhi, 2004.
17. Indian Government of Approach to Ninth Plan, Planning Commission, New Delhi, 1998.
18. Jeffery, R, Politics, *Women and Well- Being: How Kerala Became a Model*, Oxford University Press, Delhi, 2003.
19. Kabeer, N, *Reversed Realities: Gender Hierarchies in Development Thought*, Kali for Women, New Delhi, 1994.
20. Kamble, N. D., *Deprived castes and their Struggle for Equality, Ashish Publishing House,* Delhi, 1983.
21. Kothari, Rajni, *Caste in Indian politics*, New Delhi: Orient Longman, 1977. *Democratic Polity and Social Change in India,* Bombay Allied Press, Leach Edmurd, 1970.
22. Kurien Prema, 'Caste, mobility and gilding of the rituals: the impact of gultmigration on the Ezhakas of Kerala' in H. S. Verma and Nadeem Hanain (Eds.), *Stagnation, retrograde change or positive progress. Vignettes form the OBC communities in process of change,* New Delhi, Serials Publications, 2006.
23. Malik, Surendra (Eds.). *Supreme Court Mandal Commission Case*, Lucknow Eastern Book Company, 1992, SCC Suppl: 1992.
24. *Mandal Commission Report*, Vol. 1, Ch. XII, p. 55, 1979.
25. Mandal, B. P. *Report of the backward classes commission*, Vol. I to IV, Delhi the Controller of Publication, 1981.
26. Mandal, B. P., *Report of the backward classes commission,* Vol. I to IV, Government of India, Delhi, 1981.
27. Mohanty, R, 'Citizen Participation in Development: Issues of Identity, Inclusion and Voice' in Mohanty, R. and Tandon, R. (eds), *Participatory Citizenship: Identity, Exclusion, Inclusion,* Sage Publications, New Delhi, 2006.
28. Mohanty, R, 'Gendered Subjects, State and Participatory Spaces: The Politics of Domesticating Participation in Rural India' in Cornwall, A. and Coelho, V. (eds.), *Spaces for Change? The Politics of Participation in New Democratic Arenas*, Zed Books, London, 2007.

29. Omvedt, G, *Dalits and Democratic Revolution*, Sage Publications, Delhi, 1994.
30. Phillips, A, *Engendering Democracy*, Polity Press, Cambridge, 1991.
31. Phillips, A, *Which Equalities Matter*? Polity Press, Cambridge, 1999.
32. Rao, M. S. A., *Social movements among the backward classes and blacks*, 1979.
33. Ray, Renuka Report of the study team on social welfare and welfare of backward classes, Government of India, New Delhi, 1959.
34. Sarkar, S, *Writing Social History*, Oxford Univ. Press, New Delhi, 1998.
35. Shetha, D. L. and Pratp. *Empowerments of the OBC's*, Lokayan Bulletin, 13th June 1997.
36. Singh, J. P., Caste system a cultural mechanism for social and economic deprivation in H. S. Erma (Ed.), *The OBC's and the ruling classes in India*.
37. Smita Gupta, *The super panchayat outlook*, 2010.
38. Srinivas, M. N, *India: Social Structure*, Hindustan Publishing House, Delhi, 1980.
39. Srinivas, M. N, *The Village Remembered*, University of California Press, California, 1976.
40. Srinivas, M. N, *Village, Caste, Gender and Method: Essays in Social Anthropology*, Oxford University Press, Delhi, 1998.
41. Srinivas, M. N. *Caste in Modern India and Other Essays*, Asia Publishing House, New Delhi, 1962.
42. Sriram, M. S., *Nagar panchayat hospital*, Vikalpa, Vol. 26, No. 1, 2001.
43. Tamil Nadu, Government social welfare policy not Chennai. Social welfare and nutrition's meal department, Demand No. 29, 2000-2001.
44. Verma H. S. (Ed.). *The OBCs and the ruling classes in India*, Jaipur and New Delhi, Ravat Publications.
45. Verma, Neeta, *'The press and other opinion makers in the public discourses on reservation issue'* in H. S. Verma. *The OBC's and the ruing classes in India (208-230)*, Jaipur and New Delhi, Rawat Publications, 2005.
46. Young, O, *Inclusion and Democracy*, Oxford University Press, Oxford, 2000.

JOURNALS

1. "Reservation of seats for backward classes in public service and educational institutions". Journal of Indian law institute, Vol. 8, 1966, pp. 441-49.

2. Advancing class interests in the name of caste, Economic and Political Weekly, Vol. 13, No. 16, 1978.
3. Alavi Namza "Peasant" Classes and Premordical loyalties, Journal of Peasant Studies, Vol. I. No. 1. 1973, pp. 23-62.
4. Anupama Shivalingappa P. Tadasad use of gram panchayat libraries in Gulbarga district: A study SRELS, Journal of Information Management, Vol. 46: No. 1, 2009.
5. Ayyappan, "A development of tribal areas", The Economic Weekly, Vol. XVII. No. 29, 1965.
6. Beteille, A, the future of the backward classes: the competing demands of status and power; perspectives, supplement to the Indian Journal of Public Administration, 2(1), January Marcy 1965.
7. Beteille, Andre, "Empowerment"; Economics and Political Weekly, March, 6-13, 1999.
8. Blari, Harry, W. "Rising kulaks and backward classes in Bihar; Social change in the late 1970's". Economic and Political Weekly, Vol. 15, No. 2, January 12, 1980.
9. Dushkin, Lelah, "Backward class benefits and social classes in India, 1920-1970", Economic and Political Weekly, Vol. 14, 1979, pp. 661-67.
10. Dushkin, Lelah, "Caste Associations in Bangalore" Economic and Political Weekly", Vol. 15, No. 37, September 13, 1980.
11. Dushkin Lelah, "Backward class and social class in India, 1920 – 1970". Economic and Political Weekly Vol. 14, No. 14, April 7, 1979.
12. Dushkin Lelah, "Backward classes and social class in India. 1920 – 1970" Economic and Political Weekly, Vol. 14, April 7, 1979.
13. Erik Boyld, Increasing participation in democratize institutions though decentralisation empowering women and scheduled castes and tribes through panchayat raj in rural India, Democratisation, Vol. 8: No. 3, 2001.
14. George, Joseph, "Social action groups and their activities": Bangalore; centre for social action, 1998.
15. Geroge Mathew, "Panchayat Elections", Economic and Political Weekly, No. 3, 2001.
16. Ghosh – Bhola Nath, "Women Leadership in Gram Panchayat Prospects and Constraints. Journal of the Indian Anthropological – Society, 2000", 35, 1: March, 47-52.
17. M. S. Sriram, Nagar Panchayat, Hospital, Vikalpa, Vol. 26, No. 1, 2001.

18. Madhusudhan Bandhi, "Emergence of OBC leadership in Karnataka: An assessment", The Indian Journal of Political Science, Vol. LXII, No. 4, Oct. Dec., 2005, p. 890.
19. Meillaisou, Claude, "Are there castes in India", Economy and Society, Vol. 2, No. 1973.
20. N. Sreedevi, "Panchayat raj Finances in Andhra Pradesh; A macro view", Journal of Public Administration, 2007.
21. P. Praveen Sri, "Trends in Fund Flow and Utilisation of scheme funds in the panchayat raj system: A comparative analysis", Journal of Public Administration, 2007.
22. Radhakrishnan, P. "Backward class movements in Tamil Nadu". Economic and Political Weekly, 25(1), March 10, 1990.
23. Rajesh Kumar, "Political Empowerment of Weaker sections". Indian Journal of Political Science, Vol. LXIX, No. 4, Oct. – Dec. 2008, pp. 949-964.
24. "Reservation for backward castes or classes", The Economic Times, June 14, 1978.
25. Sivanna, N. "Decentralised governance and planning in Karnataka: A Historical review", Social Change, Vol. 28, No. 1, March, 1998, p. 29.
26. Srabanti Chakarvarti, Health for all though Panchayat in West Bengal: A perspective insurance chronicle, 2005.
27. Sreedevi, N. "Panchayat raj finances in Andhra Pradesh: A macro view Journal of Public Administration, 2007.
28. Subroto Dhar, "Tapping local resources to in crease panchayat incomes. Economic and Political Weekly, Vol. 41, No. 14, 2006.
29. Subroto Dhar, "Tapping Local Resources to increase Panchayat Incomes, Economic and Political Weekly, Vol. 41, No. 14, 2006.
30. Vineetha Menon: Antonyto Paul: K. N. Nair, "Dynamics of Irrigation Institutions Case Study of a Village Panchayat in Kerala", Economic and Political Weekly, 2005.
31. Viswanathan, S. "Missing Panchayat in Tamil Nadu", Front Line 2008, Vol. 25.

POLITICAL PROCESS OF BACKWARD CASTES (BCS) IN PANCHAYAT RAJ INSTITUTIONS (PRIS): PROS AND CONS - A STUDY IN ANDHRA PRADESH

QUESTIONNAIRE TO REPRESENTATIVES IN PRIS

INTERVIEW SCHEDULE

I. Socio-Economic Background of Representatives

1. Name of the Representative : ---

   District ---------------- Mandal ---------------- Gram Panchayat---------------

2. State your position and name of the place :

   a) Member of Village Panchayat b) Mandal Panchayat

   c) Zilla Panchayat

3. Are you a President or Vice President : 1. Yes 2. No

   If Yes ____________________ 1. President 2. Vice President

4. Age of the Respondent : 1. 18-25 2. 26-35 3. 36-45

   4. 45-55 5. 56 and above

5. Caste : 1. BC (A) ---------- 2. BC (B) -----

   3. BC (C) --------- 4. BC (D)-----

6. Sex : 1. Male 2. Female

7. Marital Status : 1. Unmarried

   2. Married

   3. Widow/Widower

   4. Divorced/Separated

8. Religion: 1. Hindu 2. Christian

   3. Muslim 4. Others

9. Educational Status: 1. Illiterate 2. Upto 10th 3. PUC

   4. Graduates 5. Other Specify

10. Present Occupation: 1. Agriculture 2. Coolie

    3. Business 4. Self Employer

    5. Others

11. Family Income : 1. 5,000-10,000

    2. 10,001-20,000

    3. 20,001-30,000

    4. 30,001-And above

12. Family Composition

Sl. No.	Name of the Family Members	Relationship	Sex	Age	Education	Occupation
		Husband/Wife-1 Son/Daughter-2 Grand Mother-3 Daughter-in-law /Son-in-law-4 Other Specify-5	Male – 1 Female – 2		Illiterate-1 Literate – 2 Formal Education -3	Study-1 Business-2 Self Employer-3 Agriculture-4 Coolie-5
1.						
2.						
3.						
4.						
5.						

II. Opinion towards organization and working of PRIs

1. Whether Gram sabhas are conducted regularly? 1. Yes 2. No.
2. As a representative are you attending the meetings of Gram Sabha?
   1. Yes 2. No
3. If yes give reasons
   1. ______________________
   2. ______________________
   3. ______________________
4. If no give reasons
   1. ______________________
   2. ______________________
   3. ______________________
   4. ______________________
5. Do the people attend Grama Sabha? 1. Yes 2. No
6. Do the people ask about their problems during Gram Sabha?
   1. Yes 2. No
7. Are the officials concerned attending the meeting of Gram Sabha?
   1. Yes 2. No
8. If no give reasons
   1. ______________________
   2. ______________________
   3. ______________________
9. Does Grama Sabha posses adequate powers? 1. Yes 2. No
10. If no, what are the more powers to be given?
    1. ______________________
    2. ______________________
    3. ______________________
11. In your opinion are the institutions of PR posses adequate members?
    1. Yes 2. No

12. If no, how many members the PRIs should have?
    1. ____________________
    2. ____________________
    3. ____________________
    4. ____________________
13. Is your PRI posses adequate powers to take up developmental programmes?
    1. Yes 2. No
14. If no what kind of powers do you expect?
    1. ____________________
    2. ____________________
    3. ____________________
    4. ____________________
15. Are there sufficient officials in PRIs? 1. Yes 2. No
16. Are the officials in PRIs cooperative? 1. Yes 2. No
17. If no, give reasons
    1. ____________________
    2. ____________________
    3. ____________________
18. Do you know the objectives of PRIs? 1. Yes 2. No

III. Political Process and Participation

1. Are you exercising your franchise : 1. Yes 2. No
2. Did you contest the election : 1. Yes 2. No
3. Did You Canvace in any election : 1. Yes 2. No
4. Did you mobilize the resources for any election : 1. Yes 2. No
5. Did you have any party affiliation : 1. Yes 2. No
6. Why the upper castes within BCs are being elected: ------------------------
7. Why the lower castes within BCs are not being elected: ---------------------
8. Why the upper castes within BCs will not support the lower castes: -------
9. Do find unity among the upper castes among BCs: 1. Yes 2. No
10. Why disunity among lower castes within BCs : ---------------------------

IV. Type of Participation:

1. Do you vote to your caste person : 1. Yes 2. No
   If Yes why? :
   If No why? :
2. Motivation for voting :
3. Name of the Village Leader : ------------------------- his caste -------
4. Facilitated for the improvement of your caste/family : 1. Yes 2. No
   If yes how :
   If no why? :
5. Good and bad qualities of the leader :
6. Information on the other leaders in locality :
7. Give the names of the panchayat members elected from your caste : ----------------------------
8. Their role in improving your caste :
9. Which caste has the social status among BCs: --------------------------------

10. Why : ----------------------------
11. To whom the Forward castes support: 1. BC (A) 2. BC (B) 3. BC (C) 4. BC (D)
12. Why : --------------------------------
13. Do you think that social status in more important? : 1. Yes 2. No
14. Are castes with in BCs with better economic resources and rich are able to corner the positions in PRIs : 1. Yes 2. No.
15. Give reasons : -------------------------------

IV. Development Programes :

1. Do you know what are the programes/ Schemes implemented in your village for SC, ST, OBC : 1. Yes 2. No
2. Did you got any benefits : 1. Yes 2. No
   If yes details :
   If no why :
3. Who helped you to got the benefits :
4. Whom do you blame for not getting the benefits:
5. Who benefited most in your village/ caste from the government programes? :
   Why? :
6. Are the panchayat representatives extending the benefits to their caste people? :
7. As your caste do not represent and you are not benefited from the programe : 1. Yes 2. No
8. Who are the most affected persons/ castes in your village who does not able to get govt. programmes:
   Why? ---
9. What kind of programmes are undertaken by the PRIs?
   1. ______________________________
   2. ______________________________
   3. ______________________________
10. To what extent your Panchayat has utilized the Central Govt. Schemes intended for the welfare of the SC/ST/OBC and Women?
    1. ______________________________
    2. ______________________________
    3. ______________________________
11. To what extent your Panchayat has unutilized the State Govt. Schemes intended for the welfare of the SC/ST/OBC and Women?
    1. ______________________________
    2. ______________________________
    3. ______________________________
12. What is your contribution in the making of special programmes for the benefit of the SC/ST/OBC and Women?
    1. ______________________________
    2. ______________________________
    3. ______________________________
13. How the decisions are being taken in Panchayat Raj bodies?
    1. ______________________________
    2. ______________________________
    3. ______________________________

14. How many resolutions did you move?
    1. <5 2. 5-10 3. 11-15 4. 16 and above
15. How many of them have been accepted by the body?
    1. <5 2. 5-10 3. 11-15 4. 16 and above
16. Do other members oppose your resolution? 1. Yes 2. No
17. If yes, which member is opposing?
    1. SC/ST 2. OBCs 3. GMs
18. Why they are opposing?
    1. ______________________
    2. ______________________
    3. ______________________
19. Any other information?

    ____

    ____

    ____

    ____

Index

N

Q

R

S

T

U

Z